Managing Software Requirements the Agile Way

Bridge the gap between software requirements and executable specifications to deliver successful projects

Fred Heath

BIRMINGHAM—MUMBAI

Managing Software Requirements the Agile Way

Commissioning Editor: Kunal Chaudhari

Acquisition Editor: Karan Gupta

Senior Editor: Storm Mann

Content Development Editor: Digvijay Bagul

Technical Editor: Pradeep Sahu

Copy Editor: Safis Editing

Project Coordinator: Deeksha Thakkar

Proofreader: Safis Editing

Indexer: Tejal Daruwale Soni

Production Designer: Nilesh Mohite

First published: August 2020

Production reference: 1140820

Published by Packt Publishing Ltd.
Livery Place
35 Livery Street
Birmingham
B3 2PB, UK.

ISBN 978-1-80020-646-5

www.packt.com

To my dad and mum, Mike and Rena:

All that I am, and hope to be, I owe to you

– Fred Heath

`Packt.com`

Subscribe to our online digital library for full access to over 7,000 books and videos, as well as industry leading tools to help you plan your personal development and advance your career. For more information, please visit our website.

Why subscribe?

- Spend less time learning and more time coding with practical eBooks and Videos from over 4,000 industry professionals

- Improve your learning with Skill Plans built especially for you

- Get a free eBook or video every month

- Fully searchable for easy access to vital information

- Copy and paste, print, and bookmark content

Did you know that Packt offers eBook versions of every book published, with PDF and ePub files available? You can upgrade to the eBook version at `packt.com` and as a print book customer, you are entitled to a discount on the eBook copy. Get in touch with us at `customercare@packtpub.com` for more details.

At `www.packt.com`, you can also read a collection of free technical articles, sign up for a range of free newsletters, and receive exclusive discounts and offers on Packt books and eBooks.

Contributors

About the author

Throughout his career, **Fred Heath** has worked at every stage of the software development life cycle, from writing code and designing interfaces to leading projects and dealing with clients. He has worked in a wide variety of industries, such as telecoms, defense, and education, and has experience in a plethora of programming languages and platforms. He is a Microsoft Certified Professional and Professional ScrumMaster I. Currently, he is working on developing software for the educational sector. This book is the distillation of Fred's 24 years of professional experience, including 11 years of agile development methods.

To write this book I have stood on the shoulders of giants. Ideas have seeded and taken root by names too numerous to mention here. Many thanks go to the Packt Pub editorial team for being kind and patient. A big shout out to Evadne Wu for the support and encouragement and to Steven Holdsworth and Stevie McCullough for helping test my ideas. Last, but not least, to my wife Julie and daughter Sophia for making it all worthwhile.

About the reviewer

Zack Dawood, a Canada-based technology leader, author, and speaker, has a bachelor's degree in Mechatronics Engineering from Anna University, India. He has been in the IT industry for more than 15 years and has worked in various Top Fortune 100 companies in 13 countries across Asia, Europe, and North America. He currently holds more than 35 certifications in technology and processes. The key certifications include CSM, CSPO, Certified Agile Leader, and CSP-SM from Scrum Alliance. Other certifications include SAFe Agilist, ITIL v3, Microsoft Certified Professional (Data Science), and TOGAF 9.2.

Zack is currently working as the director of consulting services at CGI Canada leading a product engineering team of 100+ members.

Packt is searching for authors like you

If you're interested in becoming an author for Packt, please visit `authors.packtpub.com` and apply today. We have worked with thousands of developers and tech professionals, just like you, to help them share their insight with the global tech community. You can make a general application, apply for a specific hot topic that we are recruiting an author for, or submit your own idea.

Table of Contents

Preface

1

The Requirements Domain

The nature of requirements and specifications	2	**A traveling analogy of goals, requirements, and specifications**	13
What is a requirement?	3	**Crossing from requirements to specifications**	14
What are specifications?	3	The requirements funnel	14
The requirements life cycle	4	The user story chaos	16
Identifying stakeholders	5	**Summary**	17
Identifying goals	7	**Further reading**	17
Domain goals	7		
Business goals	8		

2

Impact Mapping and Behavior-Driven Development

Modeling requirements with impact maps	20	**Introducing BDD**	30
Introduction to impact mapping	20	BDD with impact mapping – a perfect partnership	32
The benefits of impact mapping	21		
Identifying capabilities and features	22	**Knowing the difference between functional and non-functional requirements**	32
What is a capability?	24	**Summary**	34
What is a feature?	24	**Further reading**	35
Distinguishing capabilities from features	25		

3

Writing Fantastic Features with the Gherkin Language

What's in a feature?	38	Avoiding step repetition with	
Writing Features with Gherkin	39	Backgrounds	49
Scripting Scenarios	41	Writing a fully formed Feature	50
Discovering Scenarios	42	Tips for writing good Features	52
Avoiding repetition with Data Tables	44	Using tags to label, organize, and filter our Features	54
Adding more Scenarios	45		
Avoiding repetition with Scenario Outlines	46	Knowing why Features are executable specifications	55
Scenario Outlines versus Data Tables	48	Summary	58
		Further reading	59

4

Crafting Features Using Principles and Patterns

Applying the BDD principles	62	The composite features pattern	66
BDD isn't testing	62	The feature interpolation pattern	68
The 80-20 rule	62	Patterns to avoid	71
System behavior is not system implementation	63	Anti-pattern – thinking like developers	72
Wearing different hats	64	Anti-pattern – incidental details	73
		Anti-pattern – scenario flooding	74
Discerning patterns in our features	64	Anti-pattern – vague outcomes	74
		Anti-pattern – compound steps	76
The CRUD Features pattern	65	Summary	77

5

Discovering and Analyzing Requirements

The lost art of requirements elicitation	80	Analyzing requirements	87
Preparing for requirements analysis	82	Having a structured conversation	88
Stakeholder model	82	Decompose, Derive, Discover (D3)	89
Glossary	85	Decomposition	90

Detecting capabilities and features   91

Decomposition outcome   93

Derivation   94

Discovery   95

Business process mapping   96

Summary   99

6

Organizing Requirements

Providing easy access to our requirements model   102

Ensuring traceability with entity identifiers   103

Creating a specification document   104

Getting stakeholder agreement on the specification   106

Scoping the specification   106

Creating a product backlog   107

The Agile SDLC   107

What goes into the product backlog?   108

Where to keep the backlog   112

Summary   113

7

Feature-First Development

Setting up for successful delivery   116

Creating a staging environment   116

Creating a task board   116

Defining done   118

Actualizing just-in-time development   119

Working with Scrum   120

Sprint planning   121

Sprint development cycle   122

End of Sprint   125

Dealing with change   128

Working within Kanban   132

Kanban planning   133

Kanban development cycle   134

Dealing with change   135

Summary   135

8

Creating Automated Verification Code

Why is automated verification valuable?   138

Avoiding brittleness by layering automation code   138

The brittle step definition problem   139

Applying layers of abstraction   140

Leveraging automated
verification code patterns **142**

Hiding browser details with the
Page Object pattern 143

Wrap up complex operations with
the Façade Pattern 146

Knowing which patterns to apply
and when to apply them 147

Separating the things we verify
from the way we verify them 148

Summary **149**

9

The Requirements Life Cycle

Revisiting the requirements
management life cycle **152**

Validating requirements 153
Modeling requirements 153
Creating specifications 155
Classifying requirements 156
Documenting requirements 157
Prioritizing requirements 157
Verifying requirements 159
Dealing with change 159

Applying the Agile
requirements management
workflow **163**

Elicitation and Analysis 163
Modeling and Discovery 165
Executable specification 166
Development, Validation, and
Verification 167

Summary **168**
Further reading **168**

10

Use Case: The Camford University Paper Publishing System

Understanding the Camford
conundrum **170**

Eliciting requirements **171**

Leading the initial discussions 171
Analyzing requirements 174

Decomposing the ME's requirements 177
Deriving requirements 179
Discovering requirements 180

Planning the way forward **182**
Summary **184**

Other Books You May Enjoy

Index

Preface

Most studies in software development and project management concur that failures in requirements management are by far the most common cause of software project failure. Inaccurate or unclear requirements, a misalignment of requirements with business goals, and an inability to adapt to changes in requirements are some of the major reasons why software projects fail. This book intends to give you the weapons you need to ensure that your project avoids these pitfalls.

The aim of this book is to define, describe, and explain a clear and concise methodology, that is, a collection of rules, steps, and techniques, to help you discover, manage, and deliver requirements in an agile manner. This is achieved by applying the principles of **Behavior-Driven Development** (**BDD**) in conjunction with a number of known techniques, such as impact mapping, and some new ones, including D3 and feature-first development.

Who this book is for

This book is for software engineers, business analysts, product owners, project managers, or software project stakeholders who are looking to learn how to discover, define, model, and deliver software requirements. A fundamental understanding of the **Software Development Life Cycle** (**SDLC**) is needed to get started with this book. In addition to this, basic knowledge of the Agile philosophy and practices, such as Scrum, and some basic programming experience will be useful to get the most out of this book, but is not mandatory.

What this book covers

Chapter 1, The Requirements Domain, helps you understand the requirements domain and the difference between requirements and specifications, and introduces you to goals and stakeholders, two of the four requirements domain entities.

Chapter 2, Impact Mapping and Behavior-Driven Development, expands our knowledge of the requirements domain by defining and explaining capabilities and features. It then helps us learn how to model our requirement entities using impact maps. Finally, this chapter helps us to explore BDD and see how it complements impact mapping to provide a comprehensive requirements analysis approach.

Chapter 3, Writing Fantastic Features with the Gherkin Language, details how to define system behaviors as feature scenarios using the Gherkin language. It provides tips and techniques that will allow you to take full advantage of the expressiveness of Gherkin. It also explains how features can be leveraged as executable specifications.

Chapter 4, Crafting Features Using Principles and Patterns, offers techniques, patterns, and thought processes that will enable you to write durable and well-scoped features. It also shows you common mistakes that should be avoided.

Chapter 5, Discovering and Analyzing Requirements, teaches you three different techniques for capturing and analyzing requirements from stakeholders.

Chapter 6, Organizing Requirements, tells you what you need to do to provide transparency and traceability to stakeholders and how to get ready in order to start delivering requirements as part of an agile development cycle.

Chapter 7, Feature-First Development, illustrates how to turn features into code, using a software development process that can be applied within the Scrum framework or the Kanban method.

Chapter 8, Creating Automated Verification Code, shows you how to write solid verification code using specific design patterns.

Chapter 9, The Requirements Life Cycle, starts by outlining the techniques and methods learned in this book within the context of the canonical requirements management life cycle. Finally, it summarizes the requirements management workflow exhibited in this book.

Chapter 10, Use Case: The Camford University Paper Publishing System, recreates the beginning of a typical requirements analysis and modeling workflow using a fictional project. It also provides some tips and advice for project and client management.

To get the most out of this book

A general knowledge of software engineering is all you need to follow this book, though any working experience with Scrum or Kanban will help. The only code involved is presented in *Chapter 8, Creating Automated Verification Code*, where sample verification code in the Ruby programming language is presented.

Software/Hardware covered in the book	OS Requirements
Ruby 2.5.x	macOS X or Linux (any variant)

To run the code samples, you will need to also install the following Ruby gems (libraries): `cucumber`, `watir`, and `webdrivers`.

If you are using the digital version of this book, we advise you to type the code yourself or access the code via the GitHub repository (link available in the next section). Doing so will help you avoid any potential errors related to the copying and pasting of code.

Download the example code files

You can download the example code files for this book from your account at www.packt.com. If you purchased this book elsewhere, you can visit www.packtpub.com/support and register to have the files emailed directly to you.

You can download the code files by following these steps:

1. Log in or register at www.packt.com.
2. Select the **Support** tab.
3. Click on **Code Downloads**.
4. Enter the name of the book in the **Search** box and follow the onscreen instructions.

Once the file is downloaded, please make sure that you unzip or extract the folder using the latest version of:

- WinRAR/7-Zip for Windows
- Zipeg/iZip/UnRarX for Mac
- 7-Zip/PeaZip for Linux

The code bundle for the book is also hosted on GitHub at `https://github.com/PacktPublishing/Managing-Software-Requirements-the-Agile-Way`. In case there's an update to the code, it will be updated on the existing GitHub repository.

We also have other code bundles from our rich catalog of books and videos available at `https://github.com/PacktPublishing/`. Check them out!

Download the color images

We also provide a PDF file that has color images of the screenshots/diagrams used in this book. You can download it here: `https://static.packt-cdn.com/downloads/9781800206465_ColorImages.pdf`.

Conventions used

There are a number of text conventions used throughout this book.

`Code in text`: Indicates code words in text, database table names, folder names, filenames, file extensions, pathnames, dummy URLs, user input, and Twitter handles. Here is an example: "We put our features in files with the `.feature` extension, while our step definitions reside in files with an appropriate language extension, such as `.rb` for Ruby, `.py` for Python, `.java` for Java, and so on."

A block of code is set as follows:

```
require 'watir'
require 'webdrivers'
require 'minitest'
```

When we wish to draw your attention to a particular part of a code block, the relevant lines or items are set in bold:

```
    @browser = Watir::Browser.new
end
```

Any command-line input or output is written as follows:

```
cucumber --exclude traveler_login_[cf]
```

Bold: Indicates a new term, an important word, or words that you see onscreen. For example, words in menus or dialog boxes appear in the text like this. Here is an example: "Select **System info** from the **Administration** panel."

Tips or important notes
Appear like this.

Get in touch

Feedback from our readers is always welcome.

General feedback: If you have questions about any aspect of this book, mention the book title in the subject of your message and email us at customercare@packtpub.com.

Errata: Although we have taken every care to ensure the accuracy of our content, mistakes do happen. If you have found a mistake in this book, we would be grateful if you would report this to us. Please visit www.packtpub.com/support/errata, selecting your book, clicking on the Errata Submission Form link, and entering the details.

Piracy: If you come across any illegal copies of our works in any form on the Internet, we would be grateful if you would provide us with the location address or website name. Please contact us at copyright@packt.com with a link to the material.

If you are interested in becoming an author: If there is a topic that you have expertise in and you are interested in either writing or contributing to a book, please visit authors.packtpub.com.

Reviews

Please leave a review. Once you have read and used this book, why not leave a review on the site that you purchased it from? Potential readers can then see and use your unbiased opinion to make purchase decisions, we at Packt can understand what you think about our products, and our authors can see your feedback on their book. Thank you!

For more information about Packt, please visit packt.com.

1
The Requirements Domain

Now that we know what this book is about, we can begin our exploration of the
requirements domain. A domain is an area of knowledge within which we can operate.
As software professionals, we move between different domains daily: the coding domain,
the testing domain, as well as client-specific domains such as banking, engineering,
education, and so on. In every domain, we deal with specific domain entities that
represent items of knowledge or interactions within the domain. In the coding domain,
for instance, we deal with entities such as data structures, algorithms, functions, and so
on. These entities reflect how we capture and utilize domain knowledge. The aim of this
chapter is to introduce you to the requirements domain and its entities.

We will start by explaining the meaning of **requirements** and **specifications**, and discussing the **requirement life cycle**. We will then define the role of **stakeholders** and **actors** and talk about the goals they have in relation to our system. Lastly, we will consider the importance of bridging the gap between requirements and specifications and how this book will be approaching this problem. The main sections herein are as follows:

- The requirements domain
- Identifying stakeholders
- Identifying goals
- Goals, requirements, and specifications: a traveling analogy
- Crossing from requirements to specifications

By the end of the chapter, you will know the difference between and the importance of requirements and specifications, as well as the stages requirements move through during a project's life cycle. You will also be able to create and validate stakeholder goals, understanding the importance of writing specifications, the pitfalls with current approaches, and how this book will be tackling this subject.

The nature of requirements and specifications

Requirements can arrive at any time in the project life cycle and from a variety of people: directors, CEOs, business owners, business analysts, project managers, product owners, and end users will all at some point require or expect something of the system we are building. Our job as **system builders** is to analyze, validate, scope, and classify these requirements. We start this process by mapping requirements into a **requirements domain model**. A domain model is a representation of all the important entities and their relationships within a specific domain.

So, for instance, in the pizza-making domain (one of my favorites), we would expect to find entities such as base, toppings, restaurant, oven, and delivery person, as well as the relationships between them. Knowing what these entities are and how they are connected allows us to create and deliver pizzas. Similarly, in the requirements domain, we'd expect to find entities and relationships that help us define, conceptualize, and deliver requirements. We'll be exploring requirements domain entities and activities throughout this book.

As with every business domain, it is imperative to ensure that the **domain entities** and terms used herein are clearly defined and understood. After all, ambiguity ruins productivity and one of the goals of this book is to actualize a productive requirements management methodology, so let's start at the beginning…

What is a requirement?

Simply put, a **requirement** is a stakeholder's expression of a need, wish, or desire with regard to the system being built. Requirements come in different shapes, forms, and sizes, and from various sources. They may be provided verbally, on paper, or as computer files. Requirements may be provided as follows:

- Formal statements (for example, the system must provide a document searching facility)

- Business rules (for example, accounts with monthly deposits larger than $1,000 receive 2% higher interest)

- Examples (for example, Joe didn't have to pay for his coffee because it was his eleventh one in that store)

- User stories (for example, as a loyalty card holder)

- Business processes, that is, sets of tasks and activities that are executed in tandem in order to accomplish an organizational goal

- Screen mock-ups or wireframes

- Narratives or storyboards

- Flow-charts, activity charts, or some other type of diagram

Requirements, on their own, are not really useful. In order to be able to implement and deliver requirements, we must give them context and scope and fit them within a user workflow. In other words, we need to turn them into **specifications**.

What are specifications?

A **specification** is a description of the system behavior required in order to fulfil or realize a requirement. So, if our requirement states that *The system shall provide a document searching facility*, a specification should tell us what the system will do to allow the user to search for documents. A specification is just a way of defining how we're going to realize a requirement. Nothing more, nothing less.

Requirements without specifications are pretty useless when it comes to delivering a working system. Unless we analyze and define the impacts (that is, expected behaviors) the requirements have on our system, we stand little chance of building a system that does what its intended users want it to do. Our coding prowess, software engineering skills, and technical expertise stand for nothing unless we can build the right system. To paraphrase an old adage, *Most developers know how to build the system correctly. Not many know to build the correct system.*

Having specifications is a great start towards building the correct system. Being able to analyze and map the requirements into proper specifications is a major step towards ensuring we will be building the system that our stakeholders need and want.

The requirements life cycle

Requirements management, like many other software engineering disciplines, consists of distinct stages, as illustrated in the following diagram:

Fig. 1.1 – Requirements life cycle stages

Let's take a closer look at what each stage involves:

- **Elicitation**: The collection of requirements, which can be done in many different ways.
- **Validation**: Ensuring that the requirements fulfill a realistic and useful business need.
- **Modeling**: Having a structured and consistent way to describe and store requirements.
- **Specification**: This is where we translate the requirements into concrete and clear system behaviors.
- **Documentation**: It should go without saying that requirements must be well described, detailed, and documented.
- **Tracing**: Knowing which requirements affect system behaviors and which behaviors are necessitated by specific requirements.
- **Classification**: Requirements can be classified according to the area of the system they affect, their complexity level, their risk level, and many other factors.
- **Prioritization**: This is usually done according to impact and precedence.
- **Verification**: Ensuring that our system functions in a way that fulfills the requirements.
- **Change Management**: Dealing with changes to requirements.

Any and all of these stages may and do occur repeatedly throughout a software project's life cycle.

This book provides methods and techniques to address all of these stages. However, before we get into them, let's define and understand our requirement domain entities, starting with stakeholders.

Identifying stakeholders

A **stakeholder** is someone, or something, that derives value, benefits from, or influences our system. There is a stakeholder sub-set we call **Actors**. These are stakeholders who interact with our system, either directly or indirectly.

All actors are stakeholders, but a stakeholder is not necessarily an actor. This is because there is another sub-set of stakeholders we call **non-acting stakeholders**. These would usually be people like directors, business owners, enterprise architects, or senior managers. These usually are our business sponsors. They have a stake in the system, and they will probably make decisions that influence the system, but don't expect to see them sitting down in front of a screen and using the system any time soon. The following diagram illustrates the relationship between actors and non-acting stakeholders:

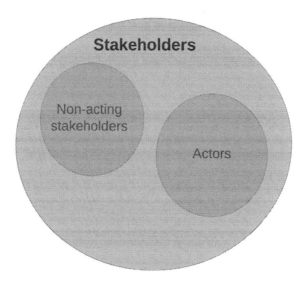

Fig. 1.2 – Stakeholders

Actors may be further divided into two categories:

- **Primary actors** interact with the system directly through a **UI** or **API** in order to achieve a specific goal.

- **Secondary actors** are actors that the system needs to be assisted by. This makes it possible to achieve the primary actor's goal.

Secondary actors may or may not have goals that they need to reach by using the system. Primary actors always have a goal that they expect to reach by using the system. Let's take the example of an online loan system. The credit consumer using the system expects to get a loan. The system will provide the loan only if it receives a positive response from a credit reference agency, such as **Experian** or **Equifax**. The credit consumer is a primary actor as they interact directly with the system in order to accomplish a specific goal. The credit reference agency is a secondary actor as the system relies on it in order to achieve the primary actor's goal.

> **Important note**
>
> System developers are not actors. Developers are an intrinsic part of the system; they act as system proxies. Actors are always external to the system.

We will be talking more about discovering and defining actors in *Chapter 5, Discovering Requirements*.

Identifying goals

Our stakeholders will have their own goals and objectives for using or sponsoring the system we are building. Understanding these goals is critical to the successful elicitation, analysis, and modeling of requirements. Stakeholder goals usually fall within two categories, depending on whether the stakeholder is a non-acting stakeholder or an actor. Actors have goals related to the domain in which they operate, for example, retail, education, and banking. Non-acting stakeholders are usually our system's business sponsors, such as directors and executives. As such, their goals are business-related; they mainly sponsor our system because they want to expand or protect their business. Let's look at domain goals first.

Domain goals

Domain goals drive our system actors to use our system in order to increase their value within their domain. For instance, if we're building a learning management system, many of its users would be aspiring to use our system to increase their knowledge or skills. If we're building a marketplace system, most of our users would want to either make money by selling items or to acquire needed items by buying them.

Here are some examples of domain goals:

- A student wants to get their coursework assessed by a teacher.
- A teacher wants to pass their knowledge on to a student.
- A teacher wants to ascertain whether the student has gained adequate knowledge.
- A seller wants to make a profit on an item they sell.
- A seller wants to get rid of an unwanted item.

As observed in these examples, an actor may have multiple domain goals. In addition, value may be added to multiple actors via the same goals. For instance, a teacher ascertaining whether the student has gained adequate knowledge benefits both the teacher and the student.

We will be exploring techniques for discovering domain goals in *Chapter 5, Discovering Requirements*. One thing to keep in mind, however, is that domain goals must always be aligned with business goals. We do not want to allow certain actors to achieve goals that could be detrimental to our business. With that in mind, let's take a closer look at business goals.

Business goals

These are goals that are mainly set by non-acting stakeholders, such as directors, VPs, and senior managers. These people are usually our executive sponsors, meaning that they may approve or support the allocation of resources and they may also champion the project to other members of senior management within the business. They do all that because they have specific goals that they want to accomplish through the adoption and use of our system. As system builders, analyzing these goals and their impact on our system is a crucial step towards defining their requirements.

A business goal's motivation and expected outcome should ultimately fall under one of these categories (see *Further reading*):

- Increasing revenue
- Reducing costs
- Protecting revenue
- Avoiding future costs

Any successful business must always be aiming towards generating enough revenue to realize its purpose. Even charities and non-profit organizations must be able to generate adequate revenue if they are to fruitfully continue their charitable or societal work.

A useful technique for determining a business goal's motivation is the **five whys technique** (see *Further reading*). If after the five questions the answer is not one of the preceding bullet points, then you should seriously question the value that a goal adds to the business. This helps to avoid and filter out vanity and pet goals, which can derail and jeopardize the project.

Consider the following business goals, where the goal's incentive can be easily discerned using the five whys:

Goal 1: *We need to automate user maintenance tasks, such as password resets and account upgrades.*

- Why? So that system users do not have to call the system administrator for routine maintenance.

- Why? So that administrators do not spend time resetting passwords and upgrading accounts.

- Why? So that administrators can spend more time monitoring the system and fixing bugs.

- Why? So that the system becomes more stable and performant.

- Why? So that we gain more users (increase revenue) and have fewer users leaving us (protect revenue).

Goal 2: *I want to reward loyal customers.*

- Why? So that returning customers can feel valued and also save some money.

- Why? So that customers keep returning more often.

- Why? So that they spend more money on our products (increase revenue).

Goal 3: *We want to receive employee feedback.*

- Why? So that the business can see what we do well and what we do badly.

- Why? So that the business can fix the bad things and keep doing the good ones.

- Why? So that our employees are happy working for the business.

- Why? So that our employees are productive and won't leave the company (avoid future costs).

Good business goals add value for stakeholders by specifying goals tangential or extrinsic to the system's inherent abilities and functionality. For instance, *I want customers to buy books* is not a valid goal for an online bookstore. For a bookstore, customers buying books is an intrinsic and implied goal. *I want customers to buy more books from us than competitor X* is better, though it still lacks a strategic aspect. With that in mind, let's take a look at strategic goals.

Strategic goals are the best goals

The best business goals are the ones that are not too abstract, nor too specific; the ones that outline strategy but not tactics. For instance, the goal *Reward loyal customers* can be framed as *Increase sales by rewarding loyal customers*. *Increase sales* is the end goal and *rewarding loyal customers* is the strategy. If the goal was simply *Increase sales* or *reduce costs* then it would ultimately fall to whoever happened to try and accomplish that goal, a business analyst or – shock, horror – a software developer to determine what the best strategy would be. The best people to define the strategy behind the goals are the non-acting stakeholders: the directors, business owners, and senior managers.

On the flipside, should the goal become something like *Increase sales by rewarding loyal customers by giving them free gift bags if they spend over $500 in a single transaction,* then we are mixing strategy with tactics. This can be a bad thing, as creating tactics requires a level of specific domain, system, and architectural knowledge that is usually lacking in non-acting stakeholders (and I'm saying this in the most respectful way). For example, the director or sales manager specifying the *free gift bag* ploy may not be aware of any logistics or distribution problems in delivering that many gift bags. Tactics are better developed by a more diverse stakeholder participation and should be captured separately as system capabilities. We will see exactly how to do this in *Chapter 2, Impact Mapping and Behavior-Driven Development.*

To put this in a military context (since it serves as a good analogy), formulating strategy is the job of the Field Marshals and Joint Chiefs of Staff. They can see the big picture and can come up with plans on how to win the war or the campaign. They create the strategy. Winning battles, on the other hand, is the job of Captains, Platoon Leaders, and other ground commanders. It is unlikely that a Field Marshal will know the specific strengths and capacity of specific platoons or have detailed knowledge of the terrain where a particular battle is to be fought, so as to create the best tactics to win the battle. These are best left to the people who have the most knowledge of such things. In a business domain, the Field Marshals are the senior business people who understand what they need to do to push the business forward. The **Captains** and **Platoon Leaders** are the project managers, architects, business analysts, and software engineers who know what to do in order to realize the Field Marshal's strategy.

Case study on lack of strategy

This business goal has a valid and obvious incentive, which is to increase revenue by increasing service contract sales.

Stated goal: *We need to increase service contract sales.*

So far so good. However, it doesn't outline a strategy for increasing service contract sales. A potential way of achieving that would be to offer the product at a discounted price if the customer also buys a service contract. Another way would be to offer customers a financial rebate if they don't raise any incidents by the end of the service contract. I am sure you can think of many other ways too. So, let's re-write the business goal with that in mind:

Offer financial incentives to customers buying service contracts.

That's better! We outlined the strategy (offer financial incentives) and we left it to the analysts, business managers, and engineers to come up with some tactics for our strategy, such as discounting product prices or offering money rebates. In the requirements domain models, we represent tactics as capabilities, and we will be examining these in detail in *Chapter 2, Impact Mapping and Behavior-Driven Development.*

Case study on specifying tactics within the goal

In this case, this business goal is about increasing revenue, which is good, but it also dictates a very specific way to achieve it.

Stated goal: *Reduce product price by 20% if customer buys a service contract.*

The trouble with this is that it constrains and limits our options in discovering any other ways to increase service contract sales. There could be more, and possibly better, ways of selling more service contracts (actually, I am certain there are). However, by sticking with this business goal we will never find out! So, let's re-write this business goal as follows:

Offer financial incentives to customers buying service contracts

This gives us the opportunity to investigate and discover all possible financial incentives we could offer in order to increase service contract sales.

The SMART trap

It is sometimes suggested that business goals follow the **SMART** criteria:

- **Specific**: Target a specific area for improvement.
- **Measurable**: Quantify or at least suggest an indicator of progress.
- **Achievable**: Ensure goal is attainable and within reach.
- **Realistic**: State what results can realistically be achieved, given available resources.
- **Time-related**: Specify when the results can be achieved.

I find strict adherence to all these criteria to be dangerous, as often the Measurable and Time-bound or Time-related criteria are too difficult to pin down in any meaningful way, especially at the beginning of a project. Even more importantly, the Measurable and Time-bound criteria can quickly turn into self-fulfilling prophecies, blinkering your organization and turning it into a quantity-driven, rather than quality-driven, business. Unfortunately, some people are unable to manage things they can't measure so they compensate by imposing artificial deadlines and random outputs. This is the kind of thinking that kills projects, as people focus on the numbers instead of the things that really matter, such as the product quality, the actual business strategy, and its clients' needs.

Eric Ries (refer to *Further reading*) calls out **vanity metrics** as non-actionable metrics that make some stakeholders feel good about themselves but do not offer any valuable insight or value. Imagine if one of our stakeholders wanted to increase sales by 50% in the next quarter. In this case, we go ahead and implement product features that cause sales to increase by 43%. Technically, we failed. In reality, though, we were a huge success. We added system functionality that caused many more people to buy our product. What if we did not hit the 50% target? Let's face it, the only reason that number existed is that *increase sales by 50%* looks much better on someone's resume than *increase sales by 43%*. It would have been much more effective if the goal was set along the lines of *Get more people to buy our product by making it easier/faster/prettier*. That would have triggered a quality-driven effort for product improvement, rather than just doing what it takes to meet an arbitrary quantity.

Case study on less time on support calls

A well-known computer manufacturer, very popular in the late 1990s, set a customer service business goal to reduce customer response time by 50%. In other words, they wanted their support staff to be able to *close* a call twice as quickly as before. The support staff reached this goal by speaking very quickly, and sometimes rudely, to their customers, not performing full diagnostics, and even hanging up on callers! The goal was achieved but a large number of consumers stopped buying computers from that company. By focusing on quantitative targets, the company degraded the quality of their service.

Case study on reducing cost, whatever the cost

A company I once worked for set a rather arbitrary but measurable and time-bound goal to reduce software department costs by a certain amount in the next year. When, towards the end of the year, costs had not been reduced by the desired amount, the directors decided to reach their goal by firing their most experienced and skilled engineers. When a new, big, and profitable project arrived some time later, the company didn't have the right staff to deliver the project. The cost-cutting target had been met but the company eventually went under. Being fixated on the metrics of their goal caused the company to make some bad strategic decisions.

Perhaps this was what famous engineer, statistician, professor, and management consultant W. Edwards Deming meant when he said this:

People fixated on meeting their targets will usually do so, even if it means destroying the company.

So, don't get obsessed with SMART goals. Instead, treat strategic business goals with valid motivations as good business goals.

> **Tip**
> Business goals are validated by ensuring they have the proper financial motivation and that they prescribe a strategy. Business goals that do neither should have their validity questioned.

A good way to understand the relationship between goals, requirements, and specifications is to think about undertaking a gastronomic expedition to a new city. Let's do that next.

A traveling analogy of goals, requirements, and specifications

Here's a thought experiment to help you to visualize the relationship between goals, requirements, and specifications. Imagine, for a moment, that you're a visitor to the great city of Cardiff in Wales, United Kingdom, and you want to sample some of the famous Welsh cakes you have heard so much about – mainly from me! So, you take out your cell phone map app and you search for the nearest Welsh cake bakery. You then ask the app for directions to the bakery. The app gives you a choice of routes dependent on your mode of transportation, the time of the day and the local traffic conditions. You then choose a route and follow it, hoping to sample some local delicacies. Let's relate this to requirements management:

- Your **goal** is to eat some Welsh cakes.
- Getting to the bakery is your **requirement**.
- The route you choose to follow is your **specification**.

It's clear that unless you have the specification (route to bakery), you will never be able to realize your requirement (get to the bakery), and achieve your goal (eat some yummy Welsh cakes!). In much the same way, unless we have a specification, we will never be able to build a system that will help our stakeholders reach their goals.

Crossing from requirements to specifications

Turning requirements into specifications is one of the hardest parts of software engineering and is the part most software engineers get wrong most often. In this section, we'll examine why this is happening and we'll set out the direction we'll be taking in this book in order to provide a safe and solid bridge between requirements and specifications.

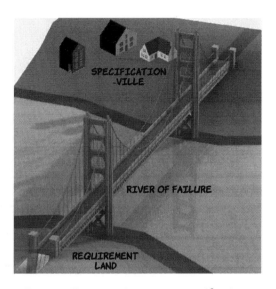

Fig. 1.3 – From requirements to specifications

We will build this bridge using a number of techniques and processes, within the context of a **behavior-driven development** (**BDD**) methodology. To understand how we will achieve this we will use a mental model called **requirements funneling**.

The requirements funnel

As system builders, we get requirements constantly thrown at us and from all directions. Our clients, but also our colleague system builders – whether they are business analysts, developers, project managers, or some other role – discover new needs, wishes, and desires, or sometimes simply change pre-discovered ones. Our job is to successfully translate these needs, wishes, or desires into specifications, either by creating new ones or mapping the requirements to existing ones. It's a bit like having a big funnel into which requirements are thrown in and, by applying certain filtering and analysis techniques, we distil them into a **requirements model** and subsequently into **executable specifications** as we can see in the following diagram. We will be talking more about executable specifications in *Chapter 3, Writing Fantastic Features*:

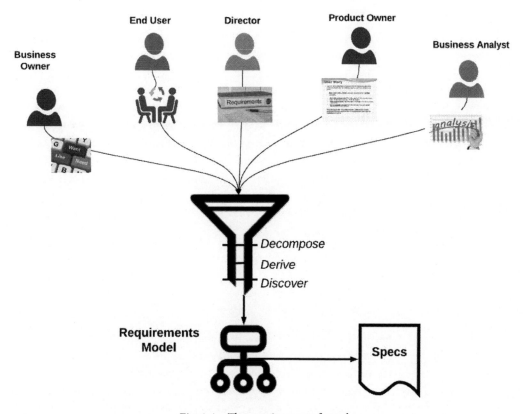

Fig. 1.4 – The requirements funnel

The filtering and analysis techniques we apply to the requirements, as they come through the funnel, are a structured conversation, business process mapping, and D3. We will examine all these in detail in *Chapter 5, Discovering Requirements*. These techniques help us produce a **Requirements Model** (**RM**). An **RM** is a well-defined, contextualized model of our system's requirements. It will be the bridge that unites our requirements with our specifications.

A common question people pose when confronted with requirements and specification analysis techniques is: *why can't I just write user stories?* Let's answer this question…

The user story chaos

As mentioned in the preface, user stories tend to be an overloaded term in the Agile and BDD worlds. Asking the question *what's a user story?* will give you a dozen different answers. A user story can be a requirement, a feature, a description, an end goal, a high-level abstraction, a small piece of business value, and many other things, depending on who you ask. This can be a source of great confusion among stakeholders as well as developers. In order to be of use to the system builders, a user story must be scoped and contextualized. However, this is rarely the case. Some people think that anything they can fit into a *As a <User>, I want to <do something> so that <I accomplish goal>* template is something that developers and analysts can take away and work with. The result is what I call *user story hell*, where our product backlog is filled with hundreds of stories, ranging in their scope from vague and abstract business needs to implementation details to bug descriptions, and many more.

User stories were always meant to be the start of a conversation about the requirements. Unfortunately, they are often used as a catch-all device for any and all ideas and desires, relevant or not. My standard response when someone asks me to create, review, or manage user stories is: *User stories for what exactly?*

More often than not, what they mean by *user story* is what in this book we refer to as a *feature*, that is, a specific entity perfectly scoped and contextualized. User stories, on the other hand, may refer to a business goal, a high-level functionality, a low-level functionality, and anything in between. Therefore, the request to *create a user story* is meaningless and moot. I find user stories to be a great way of summarizing or describing some requirements domains – particularly capabilities – (more on these in *Chapter 2, Impact Mapping and Behavior-Driven Development*) but they are not domain entities themselves. They are just structured, summary descriptions of some domain entity such as a capability or feature.

User stories are merely attributes, short descriptions of our features or other requirement domain entities, so let's not get distracted by the trees and lose sight of the forest.

> **Tip**
> Don't get hung up on user stories. They are just descriptive devices for requirements domain entities. Nothing more, nothing less. We can create perfectly solid and usable specifications without using a single user story.

As system builders, one of our responsibilities is to identify business goals and provide system capabilities that help the stakeholders accomplish their goals. We achieve this by defining and implementing features, that is, system functionality. In the next few chapters, we will learn exactly how to go about doing just that.

Summary

In this chapter, we introduced the requirements domain, explored requirements and specifications, and defined some of the main entities in the requirements domain, namely stakeholders and goals. We discussed the relationship between these entities and outlined this book's approach for bridging the gap between requirements and specifications. Being able to create valid and verifiable specifications that accurately reflect the requirements is crucial to our system's success. Understanding the requirements domain allows us to analyze and model our requirements, which is the first step towards creating a specification.

In the next chapter, we will finish our exploration of the requirements domain by talking about two more domain entities, capabilities, and features.

Further reading

- Alistair Cockburn, *Writing Effective Use Cases*, Addison-Wesley Professional, 1st Edition, 2000

- John Ferguson Smart, *BDD in Action*, Manning Publications, 1st Edition, 2014

- *Five whys*, https://en.wikipedia.org/wiki/Five_whys

- Eric Ries, https://hbr.org/2010/02/entrepreneurs-beware-of-vanity-metrics

2

Impact Mapping and Behavior-Driven Development

As well as the initial capturing of requirements, as system builders, we also need to deal with changes in requirements. A project's requirements constantly evolve, and we need to react to each stage of their evolution in two steps. The first is to correctly understand what is changing in the requirements. The second is to act on that new information in a way that helps reflect these changes and that influences the design and implementation of our system. To achieve this, we need to have a model that is a meaningful representation of our requirements.

In the previous chapter, we began to explore some of the entities within the requirements domain, namely goals and stakeholders. In this chapter, we'll expand our domain knowledge to **capabilities** and **features** and learn how to represent these four domain entities in an **impact map**. An impact map containing all the goals, stakeholders, capabilities, and features for our system is known as our system's requirements model.

Impact mapping helps us correctly identify and validate our requirements in a visual and traceable manner and it is an excellent complement to the **Behavior-Driven Development** (**BDD**) approach that we will be introducing in this chapter. BDD helps us convert our requirements into executable specifications, which can be verified against our delivered system. At the end of this chapter, we will look at the two main categories of requirements – **functional** and **non-functional** – and how they can be modeled, analyzed, and specified using impact mapping and BDD.

In this chapter, we will cover the following topics:

- Modeling requirements with impact maps
- Identifying capabilities and features
- Introducing behavior-driven development
- Knowing the difference between functional and non-functional requirements

By the end of this chapter, you will know how to distinguish capabilities from features and model basic requirements with an impact map and understand how BDD fits in with impact mapping and how we can model all types of requirements using the techniques presented in this book.

Modeling requirements with impact maps

In *Chapter 1, The Requirements Domain*, we learned how to identify **stakeholders** and **goals**. This is a crucial step in our analysis process, but in order to store and share our analytical findings, we must be able to represent these entities and their associations in a simple yet understandable manner. In other words, we want to *model* our requirement entities, and a great way of doing that is by using impact maps.

Introduction to impact mapping

Back in 2012, Gojko Adjiz defined the concept of **impact maps**, a technique that he evolved from UX-based effect-mapping methods in order to improve communication, collaboration, and interaction in teams and organizations.

Simply put, an impact map is a tree graph with four levels, where each level of the tree represents an answer to some fundamental questions about our system:

- *Why* are we building the system?
- *Who* benefits from it?

- *How* can the stakeholders achieve their goals?

- *What* can the system do to help the stakeholders achieve their goals?

This is best depicted visually, as in the following diagram:

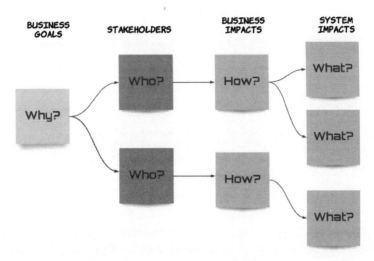

Fig. 2.1 – The meaning of an impact map

As you can see, we start by identifying a business goal (the *why*) and the stakeholders who are striving for it or are affected by it (the *who*). We then ask "*how should our stakeholders' behavior change so that the goal is accomplished?*" This is the business impact of the stakeholders trying to realize their goal. The next question is "*what can we do, as an organization or a team, to support the required impacts?*" These are the things that our organization needs to deliver to support the stakeholders' behavior. From the perspective of a software team, these are the system impacts. They are our system's features – that is, the functionality we will need to provide to the stakeholders to help them realize the business or domain impacts they need to have.

The benefits of impact mapping

Impact mapping brings some very distinct advantages to the requirements management table:

- **Focus**: By clearly answering the *why, who, what,* and *how* questions, a requirement inevitably raises – we can focus exactly on the area we need to work on, clarify, or elaborate upon.

- **Traceability**: Stakeholders have goals and they create impacts that can be delivered via our system by implementing features. At any time, we can see what we're doing, how and why we're doing it, and who's going to benefit from it.

- **Readability**: Impact maps can be easily (and ideally) presented as mind maps or tree graphs. They provide a visual, easy-to-understand representation of our requirements model.

- **Collaboration and interaction**: Each level of the impact map should ideally be filled with the participation and collaboration of different people: business people for the *why*, developers for the *what*, and so on. This fosters cooperation and collaboration between people that wouldn't otherwise interact with each other.

- **Strategic vision**: By aligning our targets, features, and activities with the business objectives and the business objectives with the stakeholders, we help everyone see the big picture and make better roadmap decisions.

Over the years, I have found impact mapping to be a wonderfully effective way of modeling and visualizing requirements. The analytical process involved in impact mapping is also an ideal complement to the BDD methodology, which we will be discussing over the next few pages. But before we do that, let's complete our knowledge of the requirement domain entities by examining capabilities and features and how they fit into our impact mapping model.

Identifying capabilities and features

In *Chapter 1*, *The Requirements Domain*, we identified two of the main entities in the requirements domain: **stakeholders** and **goals**. In the previous section about impact mapping, we saw how these entities slot perfectly into an impact map. It's time now to look at the other two main entities that constitute the requirements domain and how they are all represented within an impact map.

In the *Introduction to impact mapping* section earlier in this chapter, we saw how the third and fourth levels of an impact map correspond to the business and system impacts of a stakeholder's effort to accomplish their goal, respectively. We shall define the business impact as a **capability**. A capability is a stakeholder's required ability to do something with our system in order to reach their goal. We shall define the system impact as a **feature**. A feature is a system functionality or behavior required in order to support a capability. Let's now look at the impact map once more in light of these new definitions:

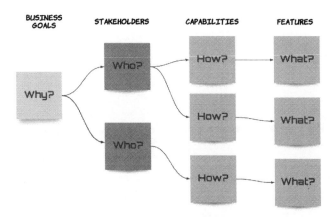

Fig. 2.2 – Requirements domain model as an impact map

As illustrated in the preceding diagram, we can use impact mapping to build a requirements model. We have represented all four of our core requirement domain entities and their relationship to one another:

- **Goal (why)**: The intended benefit of our system
- **Stakeholder (who)**: Someone who interacts with, benefits from, or is otherwise affected by our system
- **Capability (how)**: A system ability that enables stakeholders to achieve a goal
- **Feature (what)**: A functionality that helps support a capability

As shown here, the key differentiation between capabilities and features is that the **capabilities** are discovered by answering the question "*how can the stakeholder accomplish their goal?*", while **features** are discovered by answering the question "*what functionality must the system provide in order to deliver these capabilities to the stakeholders?*"

> **Important note:**
> Some people use the terms **high-level features** and **low-level features**, or features, epics, and user stories, to denote the meaning of capabilities and features. To avoid confusion, to keep things tightly focused, and also to avoid the user story conundrum (see the *User story chaos* section of *Chapter 1, The Requirements Domain*), we'll be using the term **capability** to describe a high-level impact and the term **feature** to describe a lower-level functionality needed to deliver that capability.

Since we've already defined and discussed business goals and stakeholders in *Chapter 1, The Requirements Domain*, let's now take a look at what capabilities and features are in more detail.

What is a capability?

A capability is a system ability that enables a stakeholder to achieve a goal. It encapsulates the *impact* that the stakeholder has on our system in order to successfully realize their goal. Capabilities reflect domain- or business-level requirements that don't describe or prescribe a particular implementation. Here are some capability examples:

- **Example 1**: Sarah is a seller on a marketplace app. Her goal is to sell her items as quickly as possible. To achieve her goal, she needs the capability to make her stock more visible to buyers.

- **Example 2**: Tom is a seller on a marketplace app. He wants to empty his house of bulky items he no longer needs. To achieve this goal, he wants the capability to offer buyers a discount if they can pick up the item from his house.

- **Example 3**: Jane is the CTO of the company that builds the marketplace app. One of her goals is to increase the number of people using the app. To achieve her goal, she needs the capability to offer new visitors to the website incentives to make them register as members.

Capabilities define *how* our stakeholders will impact our system's behavior, but not *what* the system behavior will be. Our job as system builders is to support and deliver these capabilities. We do this by implementing features.

What is a feature?

A feature describes a system behavior. It's closely associated with a capability and answers the question "*what system functionality do we need to implement in order to deliver this capability?*" If a capability represents the impact the stakeholder has on our system, then a feature represents the impact that capability has on the development team. Features describe the system behavior, not its design or architecture. In other words, they describe what the system does, from an actor's perspective. Features are described in business domain terminology and are usually structured in the form of a title, some descriptive information or a user story, and a number of acceptance criteria (we'll be referring to those as **scenarios**). Let's take a look at some examples of features:

- **Example 1**: Sarah is a seller on a marketplace app, who needs the capability to make her stock more visible to buyers. Some features that could help support this capability are placing Sarah's stock on top of the stock listings and sending marketing emails about Sarah's stock to prospective buyers.

- **Example 2**: Tom is a seller in a marketplace app, who wants the capability to offer buyers a discount if they can pick up the item from his house. A feature that would support this capability is adding money-off stickers to Tom's items for sale, promoting this discount.

- **Example 3**: Jane is the CTO of the company that builds the marketplace app. She requires the capability to offer incentives to new visitors to the website in order to make them register as members. Displaying the membership benefits, such as free delivery, at the users' checkout is a feature that would help realize this capability.

We now have a basic understanding of features, and we'll be talking much more about them in *Chapter 3, Writing Fantastic Features with the Gherkin Language.*

Distinguishing capabilities from features

The distinction between capabilities and features can sometimes seem artificial. There are, however, some easy ways of distinguishing between the two. The main distinction is that they each answer different questions:

- **Capability**: How can the stakeholder accomplish their goal within our system? Another way of putting it would be *what impact does the stakeholder need to have on the system in order to accomplish their goal?*

- **Feature**: What does the system need to do in order to provide the capability the stakeholder needs? As system builders, what functionality must we implement so that the stakeholder will have this capability?

In summary, the following criteria can also be used to distinguish between capabilities and features:

	Capability	Feature
Granularity	Coarse	Fine
Atomicity	Transactional	Atomic
Key action	Enable	Provide
Key question	How	What
Point of view	Stakeholder	System
Association	Goal	Capability
Directly actionable	No	Yes

Fig. 2.3 – Distinction between capabilities and features

Let's examine these criteria in more detail:

- **Granularity**: Capabilities are sky-level entities. They describe impacts as viewed from a high vantage point – for instance, *publishing articles*. They don't specify system details or specific system behaviors. Features are ground-level entities. They describe specific system functionalities, such as *user sets their profile* or *author creates article.*

- **Atomicity**: A capability usually encapsulates a complete business process, which is an end-to-end, structured, and sequential set of activities that – when applied correctly in their entirety – will accomplish a goal. A feature, on the other hand, represents an atomic activity, or a sub-set of activities, that usually isn't enough by itself to achieve a goal.

- **Key action**: A capability can be thought of as *enabling* the stakeholder to do something with our system in order to achieve their goal. A feature is about our system *providing* the stakeholder with some functionality so that they are able to do that thing that allows them to achieve their goal.

- **Key question**: As previously stated, capabilities answer the question of "*how can we help a stakeholder accomplish their goal?*" Features answer the question of "*what does the system need to do in order to deliver a capability?*"

- **Point of view**: A capability is always viewed from the stakeholders' point of view. Actually, user stories are a great way of describing capabilities – for example, "*as a graduate student, I want to be able to publish my thesis so that I can get it reviewed by the examiners.*" A feature is discovered by looking at a capability from a system's point of view – that is "*As the system, what functionality must I provide to the graduate student so that they can publish their thesis?*"

- **Association**: A capability is always directly related to a goal. If a stakeholder's goal is to eat a pizza, then they should be able to *select toppings*, *book a delivery slot*, or have other capabilities. If any of these capabilities is absent, the stakeholder may not be able to get their pizza – that is, they won't be able to accomplish their goal.

- **Directly actionable**: A feature is directly actionable – that is, a developer can take it away and start working on it with only a few questions. A capability is not usually directly actionable, so a developer cannot start working on it without asking many questions about what the capability involves and how it can be delivered.

Having clarified those differences, let's take a look at some examples of identifying features and capabilities.

Use case 1 – Content rating requirements for a knowledge-sharing platform

In this use case, we are building a knowledge-sharing platform where software developers can exchange tips, advice, and other forms of knowledge. Many developers posting blog posts on our platform tell us that they would like to have their posts rated by other developers so that they can build up a reputation as knowledgeable and effective developers.

Here, the domain goal is to increase posters' reputations. In order to accomplish this goal, blog posters need to be able to have their content rated by blog readers. This is a capability that can be easily identified as it directly relates to a goal. It's also coarsely grained and answers the question of how to accomplish a stakeholder's goal. The next step is to try to derive some features that will help us deliver this capability. To do that, we – the system builders – need to communicate with both the posters and readers about the best ways we can support this capability. After doing so, we come up with two pieces of functionality:

1. Use a star-rating system, where the reader gives a post a rating of 1 to 5 stars, depending on how useful they thought the post was.

2. Enter textual feedback, where the reader can add some comments about the things they liked or didn't like in the post.

These two ways of delivering the capability are our features. We can model the entities we have captured in the diagram here:

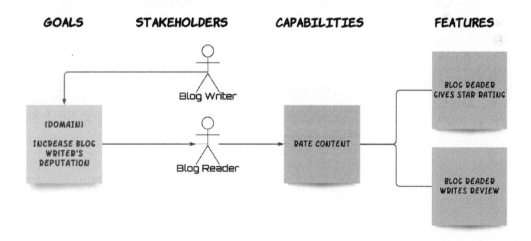

Fig. 2.4 – Requirements modeling for the content rating use case

There are a couple of things of note in this diagram.

First of all, an actor's goal is being realized through another actor's impact. To help the blog writer reach their goal, we need to provide a blog reader with the capability to rate the blog writer's content.

The main actor involved in this capability – that is, the blog reader – does not have an inherent goal to realize by leveraging the capability. They are in fact helping another actor realize their own goal. This is absolutely fine. In fact, cases like these help us explore the domain more and discover new goals and capabilities. So, in this case, we could ask ourselves "*how can we encourage blog readers to write more reviews?*" We could easily discover that we need additional capabilities, such as awarding badges for readers who write the most reviews.

Use case 2 – onboarding new employees

In this use case, we are working on a new **Human Resources (HR)** management system for our organization. Our HR director tells us that they want our new HR system to facilitate the onboarding of new employees. The onboarding business process requires new hires to be allocated a company identification number, to provide some personal information, and be given the company manuals and procedure documents.

We can deduce (and confirm with the HR director) that the business goal they want to accomplish here is to automate the onboarding process so as to save staff time and company money. *Onboarding new employees* is a capability because it is coarsely granular and describes something that the actor needs to be able to do in order to achieve the *reduce staff work* goal. *Provide new employee with an employee ID*, on the other hand, captures a feature because it is very specific – it answers the question "*how can the system implement new employee onboarding?*" and doesn't by itself produce a tangible result. The same reasoning can be applied to conclude that *preview company manuals and procedures* and *capture employee details* are also features. We can model this analysis as an impact map in the following diagram:

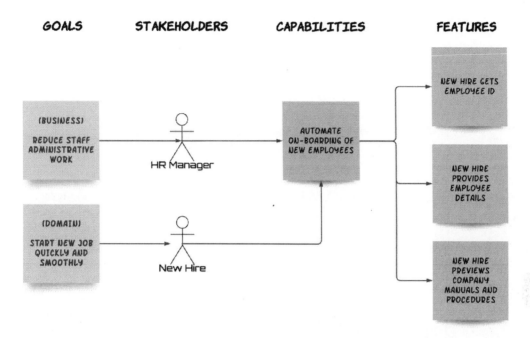

Fig. 2.5 – Requirements modeling for the HR management system use case

You may notice that we have also defined a goal for our new hire actor. The same capability often serves the purposes of more than one stakeholder, usually both actors and non-acting stakeholders, and can help achieve both business and domain goals (we talked about different goals in the *Identifying goals* section of *Chapter 1, The Requirements Domain*). The HR manager needs to have this capability available to system users in order to reduce HR staff administrative work. The new hire needs this capability for themselves in order to start their new working experience as quickly and smoothly as possible

> **Tip**
> It is important to identify other stakeholders and goals associated with a capability. This helps us discover more capabilities, features, and stakeholders that we might not have otherwise discovered.

We will be exploring patterns for discovering capabilities and features in later chapters. In the meantime, let's take a look at a very important paradigm that underpins the methodology described in this book: BDD.

Introducing BDD

In this section, we will be introduced to **BDD**, as it forms an essential part of the methodology described in this book. BDD was first introduced as a concept by Dan North back in 2006 (refer to *Further reading link #2*), as a way to improve communication and collaboration and to facilitate behavior-based automated testing. BDD is often referred to as an *outside-in* development methodology, as it focuses on system behavior required by the stakeholders as the driving mechanism for developing software. This well-defined system behavior is referred to as a **feature** in BDD parlance.

Since North's original article, BDD has matured and evolved and now has a rich ecosystem supporting it, with tools such as Cucumber, SpecFlow, and JBehave appearing in many a developer's tool-belt. Gojko Adjiz (yes, him again) helped solidify BDD principles in his book *Specification by Example* (refer to *Further reading link #4*). As a result, some people actually use the terms BDD and *specification by example* interchangeably.

The BDD approach is illustrated in the following diagram:

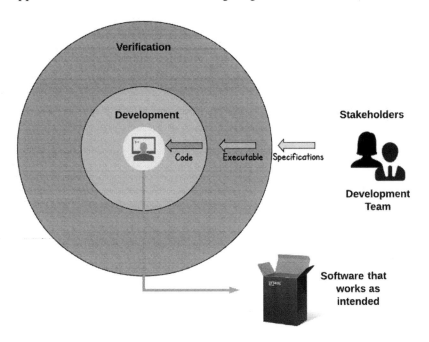

Fig. 2.6 – BDD life cycle

As we can see in the preceding diagram, while traditional development methods require the developer to write some code, which then gets verified and released, BDD inverses the paradigm by having the stakeholders and the development team come together to create executable specifications before writing code.

The BDD life cycle involves three stages:

1. The stakeholders and the development team come together to create the **specifications**. The specifications are, in effect, our features as described in the *What is a feature?* section of this chapter. Features are our system behaviors written in plain domain language that everyone can read and understand. Specifications are features analyzed in detail and written in a structured, prescribed manner. We will fully examine how to write our features and create specifications in *Chapter 3, Writing Fantastic Features with the Gherkin Language*.

2. The development team writes executable code for our specifications. This is code that runs within our system and exercises the behaviors specified in our features. Let's suppose that our specification says something like "*when the user logs in using the correct username and password, they see a welcome message.*" The development team will write some code that brings up the login screen, logs in with the correct credentials, and checks that a welcome message does indeed show on the screen. That way, we can actively verify that our system does what we agreed it's going to do. This is why in BDD we talk about **executable specifications**. It is because our specified system behavior is executed and verified as part of the BDD life cycle.

3. After the executable part of the specification is written, the development team can produce the actual system code. They will know when they've written the right code because they will be using the executable specification to verify the system that they are producing.

We will be discussing BDD, features, and specifications in great detail in *Chapter 3, Writing Fantastic Features with the Gherkin Language*. But first, let's discover how BDD and impact mapping form an ideal match.

BDD with impact mapping – a perfect partnership

By looking at the BDD diagram in *Fig. 2.6*, you may have noticed that the BDD life cycle begins with the establishment of some specifications, which is the discovery and creation of some features. However, BDD does not prescribe any specific way of discovering these features. Most BDD books and proponents advocate different ways of formulating user stories after communicating with the stakeholders. However, leveraging user stories as a means of capturing requirements and translating them into specifications can be vague, risky, and confusing, as we already discussed in the *User story chaos* section of *Chapter 1, The Requirements Domain*.

This is where impact mapping, in conjunction with some other techniques described in the *Discovering requirements* section of *Chapter 4, Crafting Features Using Principles and Patterns*, comes into its own. Using these techniques alongside impact mapping, we can safely and reliably capture, analyze, and model our requirements, as well as create our system specifications. Once we have our specifications, we can start applying our standard BDD development life cycle and reap the benefits of producing a system that works as our stakeholders expect, the first time and every time!

But before we delve more into features, let's see how BDD and impact mapping help us deal with different types of requirements.

Knowing the difference between functional and non-functional requirements

Let's now take a look at the main type of requirements we are going to encounter and how we will be dealing with them. In the use cases and examples we have used so far, we have encountered requirements that influence what the system should do or how it should behave. In our pizza example, we talked about the actors selecting toppings for the pizza, choosing a delivery slot, and other such functionalities or behaviors. These are commonly known as **functional requirements** and we've already seen how we can represent these in a requirements model by identifying goals, stakeholders, capabilities, and features. But let's now consider some different requirements that don't focus on interactions between the system and its actors but on internal system operations instead: **Non-Functional Requirements (NFRs)**.

Let's suppose that the pizza company wants our system to display all 50 available toppings to the user within 2 seconds; otherwise, the customer will get bored and go order their pizza from somewhere else. They also want the customer to be able to order their pizza from their desktop computer, tablet, and cell phone. These requirements don't affect what our system will be doing but *the way it should be doing it*. NFRs are requirements that focus on the operational, rather than the behavioral, aspect of a system. They are sometimes referred to as **constraints** or **quality attributes**. The most common areas for NFRs are as follows:

- Performance
- Security
- Scalability
- Authentication and authorization
- High availability
- Responsiveness
- Internationalization and localization
- Cross-platform compatibility
- Compliance
- Accessibility

NFRs are very important as they often are what **Service Level Agreements (SLAs)** are based on. SLAs usually specify constraints for the system's availability, performance, and responsiveness. SLAs are contractually binding items, so being able to define, model, and verify them as part of our methodology provides us with extra confidence in our system delivery. The great thing is that we can still model NFRs in the usual manner by defining stakeholders, goals, capabilities, and features. When our pizza shop wants our system to display all 50 available toppings to the user within 2 seconds, what they are looking for is a **high-performance capability**. This kind of capability is usually associated with business goals such as *increase/retain customer base*. After all, if our system is slow or unresponsive, our customers will be ordering their pizza somewhere else and we definitely don't want this to happen. We could phrase this capability as a user story:

As the pizza shop owner, I want the online system to be performant so that existing customers can finish placing their order quickly.

We can capture all performance-related constraints as features required to deliver the *high-performance* capability, as depicted in the following impact map:

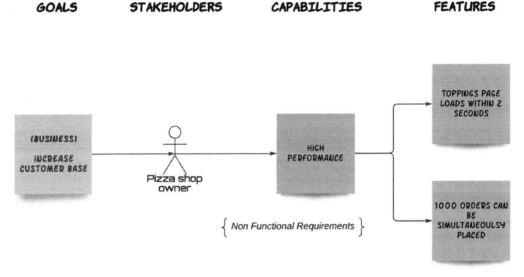

Fig. 2.7 – NFR requirement impact map

Once we have identified the high-performance capability, we can discuss with our stakeholders other potential ways of delivering it. We can hence identify new features, such as allowing many orders to be placed simultaneously without loss of performance, as depicted in the preceding diagram. Actually, when dealing with NFRs, we can use a technique other than simply creating new capabilities and features. We will talk about this in *Chapter 4, Crafting Features Using Principles and Patterns*, when we discuss features in greater detail.

Summary

In this chapter, we defined and distilled two more requirement domain entities: **capabilities** and **features**. We learned how to use them alongside **goals** and **stakeholders** in order to model our requirements in a requirements model, using impact mapping. Knowing what these four entities are about and how they are related is the first step in the requirements management workflow that we'll be detailing in this book. We already started exploring the mental process we'll be using to analyze requirements and break them down into these four entities. We'll be delving in greater detail into how this mental process works in *Chapter 5, Discovering and Analyzing Requirements*, in the *Discovering Requirements* section, where we will also be applying effective techniques to help us discover and analyze requirements.

This chapter also introduced BDD. BDD is what we do after we have discovered and analyzed our requirements. Specifically, BDD will help us refine our requirements and turn them into specifications – that is, features. In the last section of this chapter, we talked about different types of requirements. Knowing which kind of requirement you are dealing with will help you determine and apply the best techniques to model, analyze, and implement it.

In the next chapter, we will be getting into the nitty-gritty of BDD by learning how to correctly write features. This is where it's starting to get real, so stay tuned for some interesting and exciting stuff!

Further reading

1. Gojko Adzic, *Impact Mapping: Making a Big Impact with Software Products and Projects*, ISBN-10: 0955683645

2. Dan North, *Introducing BDD*: `https://dannorth.net/introducing-bdd`

3. John Ferguson Smart, *BDD in Action: Behavior-driven development for the whole software lifecycle, Manning Publications, 1st edition*, ISBN-10: 161729165X

4. Gojko Adzic, *Specification by Example: How Successful Teams Deliver the Right Software, Manning Publications, 1st edition*, ISBN-10: 1617290084

    Mike Cohn, *User Stories*: `https://www.mountaingoatsoftware.com/agile/user-stories`

3
Writing Fantastic Features with the Gherkin Language

In the previous chapter, we discussed capabilities and features and we learned how to define and model them using *Impact Maps*. We also introduced **Behavior-Driven Development (BDD)** and discussed how it's centered around features. In this chapter, we'll build on this knowledge by talking *exclusively* about **Features**. We'll discover how to write them correctly, how to accurately specify system behavior with **Scenarios**, and what makes our `Features` executable specifications that can be used to automate our system's verification. Features being written incompletely or inaccurately will mean that our system's behavior will not be properly conveyed to our **stakeholders**, which is the pre-cursor to ambiguity, misinterpretations, and – ultimately – project failure. In this chapter, we will make sure that this doesn't happen.

In particular, we will cover the following:

- What's in a feature?
- Writing `Features` with Gherkin
- Scripting `Scenarios`
- Knowing why `Features` are executable specifications

After reading this chapter, you will know all about `Features`: their structure, content, and usefulness.

What's in a feature?

As mentioned in *Chapter 2*, *Impact Mapping and Behavior-Driven Development*, specifically the *Capabilities and Features* section, a **feature** is a functionality implemented by our system in support of a capability. At a minimum, a feature consists of a **Feature Title** and a **Scenario**. A scenario is a look at the feature's functionality from a specific perspective. So, if our feature is titled *Bank customer withdraws cash from cash machine*, for instance, we could have scenarios such as *Not enough cash in machine* or *Bank note denominations don't match requested amount*.

However, having just a title and a scenario doesn't help us describe the whole functionality. A fully formed feature will include the following:

- **Feature Title**: A brief description of the presented functionality – for example, *Bank customer withdraws cash from cash machine*.
- **User Story**: Most people use the following template:

  - As an [Actor]

  - I want [specific system behavior]

  - So as to achieve [a goal contributing to a Capability]
- **Impact**: A link to the impact map this feature relates to.
- **Notes**: Any other text that helps the reader better understand the feature.
- **Background** (if applicable): A prerequisite or `condition` common across all scenarios.

- **Scenarios**: A descriptive feature will have *several scenarios*, which are written in a structured manner:

  Given [a Condition]

  When [an Action is invoked]

  Then [an expected Outcome occurs]

Features serve two purposes:

- They specify system behavior in a clear and structured manner so that they can be read and understood by any and all stakeholders.

- They allow system behavior to be verified against system releases and deployments by using automation tools that match system behaviors to verification code.

> **Tip**
>
> If a stakeholder cannot – or will not – read a Feature because it is too long or complicated, or contains technical jargon, then *that feature is useless*. The main purpose of a feature is to be read. If the structure or language of the feature hinders or prevents readability, then that feature is not fit for purpose!

Features are not written as free or unstructured text. We write Features using a specific structure and following certain rules. In fact, there is a whole domain language just for writing Features. Let's take a look at it.

Writing Features with Gherkin

We write Features in a structured manner, using a natural language subset called **Gherkin** (https://cucumber.io/docs/gherkin/reference/). Gherkin documents, such as a feature file, are written in a specific syntax. Most lines in a Gherkin document start with a keyword, followed by our own text. These keywords are as follows:

- Feature
- Rule (as of Gherkin version 6)
- Scenario (or example)
- Given, When, Then, And, *

- Background
- Scenario Outline (or Scenario Template)
- Example

Comments are only permitted at the start of a new line, anywhere in the feature file. They begin with zero or more spaces, followed by a hash sign (#) and some text. Gherkin supports over 70 languages, from Arabic to Uzbek, so we can write our Features in any language we choose.

A Feature's outline is as follows:

```
Feature: My Beautiful Feature # The Feature title

## We can write anything we want from here until the next
keyword
## As suggested in the previous section we should put here the
following:
## -- User Story: a description of our feature
## -- Impact: a link to our Impact Map for this feature
## -- Notes to help readers understand the Feature

Background: # (optional) a common Condition which applies to
all scenarios
Scenario: # a specific behavior of our Feature
Scenario: # another behavior of our Feature
## ...more Scenarios
```

Feature should tell its readers all that they need to know in order to understand how the system will behave when that specific functionality is exercised. Variation in Feature's behavior is described by using different Scenarios.

Scenarios are written in the following manner:

```
Scenario: The Scenario Title
Given <a Condition>
And <another Condition>
And ....
When <an Event or Action takes place>
And <another Event or Action takes place >
And ....
```

```
Then <an expected Outcome occurs>
And <another expected Outcome occurs >
And ….
```

As you can see, Scenario has a title. As Feature may comprise many Scenarios, it is important that each Scenario has a descriptive title. A **Scenario** specifies system behavior in terms of Conditions, Events, or Actions and Outcomes. Each Condition, Event/Action and Outcome consists of one or more **steps**, described in a single line of text. Each step is atomic; that is, it specifies a single Condition, Event/Action, or Outcome in its entirety. To specify multiple Conditions, Events/Actions, or Outcomes, we may use conjunctions such as *And*, *Or*, and *But* at the beginning of a new step.

All Scenarios are structured in the same way: Given some conditions, When certain events or actions take place, Then specific outcomes should occur. This structure makes it easy to accurately specify our system's behavior while also facilitating the creation of executable steps, as we shall see in the *Features are executable specifications* section, later in this chapter.

In the following sections of this chapter, we'll examine good and bad practices when writing Features and Scenarios. Let's begin by digging deeper into writing Scenarios...

Scripting Scenarios

Scenarios are a feature's essence. They reflect the change in the feature's behavior under different circumstances. We call this section *Scripting Scenarios* as Scenarios are written similarly to a stage play or film script. They are written using prompts and specific actions for particular actors. Before we discuss how to script our Scenarios, let's see how we can discover them first…

Discovering Scenarios

A good way to visualize scenarios is by using the metaphor of a Rubik's cube. Imagine that your feature is a Rubik's cube. You have it in your hands and you turn it around, looking at it from different angles. You notice how each side has different colors in different arrangements. It's the same cube, but each time you turn it, you discover some new image patterns and cell arrangements:

Feature

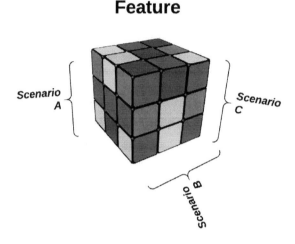

Fig. 3.1 – Feature as a Rubik's cube

When discovering `Scenarios`, we follow a similar mental process. We look at our `Feature` from different angles and perspectives. `Feature` itself doesn't change; it remains a piece of system functionality that contributes toward a capability. What changes is how that functionality adapts to different circumstances. Let's look at an example:

- `Feature Title`: The author uploads a picture to their profile.

- `Notes`: The author needs to have a profile picture so that readers can relate to them on a more personal level.

Every `Feature` will have at least one **Happy Path Scenario**. This is the `Scenario` where the `Feature`'s main actor accomplishes the feature's objective without any hindrance. Some people call this the *blue sky* or *best-case* scenario. In our `Feature` example, the `Happy Path Scenario` may look like this:

```
Scenario: Happy Path
Given the user is logged in as an Author
And the Author goes to their Profile page
And the Author chooses to upload a picture
```

```
When the Author selects an image file from their computer
And the Author uploads the file
Then the Author sees their uploaded image as their Profile
picture
```

This is a `Scenario` where all our assumptions were correct. *"Which assumptions were these?"* I hear you ask! Well, in this `Scenario`, we implicitly assumed the following:

- The `Author` will be uploading a file stored on their computer.
- The `Author` can choose any type of image file.
- The system allows any size of image file to be uploaded.

It is now time to twist and turn that Rubik's cube and look at our `Feature` from different angles, where our assumptions are not valid. After consulting with our development team, we find out that not all image file types can be treated the same way (for various technical reasons). Furthermore, we are told that high-resolution images take up a lot of storage and should be avoided. At the same time, images below a certain resolution will not have enough clarity to be used as a profile picture. If you remember, back in *Chapter 2, Impact Mapping and Behavior-Driven Development*, we talked about **Non-Functional Requirements (NFRs)**. This is such a case where these NFRs trickle into our features and start influencing our scenarios. In order to reflect these newly found constraints, we re-write our *Happy Path Scenario* as follows:

```
Scenario: Successful image upload
Given the user is logged in as an Author
And the Author goes to their Profile page
And the Author chooses to upload a picture
When the Author selects an image file from their computer
And the file is of type:
| file-type |
| jpg |
| gif |
| png |
And the file is of a size less than  "5 " MB
And the file is of a resolution higher than  "300 " by  "300 "
pixels
And the Author uploads the file
Then the Author sees their uploaded image as their Profile
picture
```

> **Tip**
>
> When we look at a `Happy Path Scenario` and try to imagine what happens when our assumptions and constraints do not apply, we say that we *invert* the `Scenario`. `Scenario` inversion is a great way to discover more `Scenarios`.

You may have noticed that we changed our Scenario's title from the generic *Happy Path* to the more descriptive *Successful image upload*. We sometimes get to have more than one *Happy Path Scenario* within our `Feature`, so it's good practice to give each scenario a meaningful name. Let's take a look at one other way with which we improved our `Feature`...

Avoiding repetition with Data Tables

When we specified the *file type* step in our preceding scenario, we used a list with the acceptable file types. This list is actually a one-column table. The Gherkin language allows us to do that so that we can avoid the repetition of steps. We could have said this:

```
And the file type is jpg
Or the file type is gif
Or the file type is png
```

We used a `Data Table` instead:

```
And the file is of type:
  | file-type |
  | jpg |
  | gif |
  | png |
```

The first row of our table is the **header row**. The next three rows are the **data rows**. Using `Data Tables` makes our scenario neater and easier to read. Although in this instance we are using a one-column table, in reality, we could have many columns (and rows) in a Data Table.

Adding more Scenarios

In creating our *Happy Path Scenario*, we identified the necessary constraints in order to successfully upload a profile picture. These are as follows:

- The `Author` will be uploading a file stored on their computer.
- The `Author` can choose any type of image file.
- The system allows any size of image files to be uploaded.

Now let's capture our system's behavior when those constraints are broken, by adding some more `Scenarios`:

```
Scenario: Wrong type of image
Given the user is logged in as an Author
And the Author goes to their Profile page
And the Author chooses to upload a picture
When the Author selects an image file from their computer
And the file is of type:
  | file-type |
  | svg |
  | tiff |
  | bmp |
Then the Author sees a message informing them that the file
type is not supported
And the file is not uploaded
```

In the preceding `Scenario`, we try to upload some unsupported files. The expected outcome is that the system informs us of the file type incompatibility. Now let's add a new `Scenario` to capture our system's behavior when trying to upload large files:

```
Scenario: Image too large
Given the user is logged in as an Author
And the Author goes to their Profile page
And the Author chooses to upload a picture
When the Author selects an image file from their computer
```

```
And the file is of type:
| file-type |
| jpg |
| gif |
| png |
And the file is of size greater than   "5 " MB
Then the Author sees a message informing them that the file is
too big
And the file is not uploaded
```

In this Scenario, the file type we are uploading is acceptable, but its image resolution isn't, so we expect a system error message. Because we expect the system to refuse uploading a file over a certain size, regardless of its file type, we can actually skip the file type step definition altogether:

```
Scenario: Image too large
Given the user is logged in as an Author
And the Author goes to their Profile page
And the Author chooses to upload a picture
When the Author selects an image file from their computer
And the file is of size greater than   "5 " MB
Then the Author sees a message informing them that the file is
too big
And the file is not uploaded
```

This makes it clear to our Feature readers that, in this specific Scenario, we don't care about file types. The only criterion for failure here is the file size. Now let's take a look at creating a scenario to capture the image resolution constraint.

Avoiding repetition with Scenario Outlines

We were told by our development team that the picture resolution must be a minimum of 300 pixels wide by 300 pixels high; otherwise, the picture won't be clear enough. We can go ahead and write a Scenario that captures this constraint:

```
Scenario: Resolution too low
Given the user is logged in as an Author
And the Author goes to their Profile page
And the Author chooses to upload a picture
When the Author selects an image file from their computer
```

```
And the file is of type:
| file-type |
| jpg |
| gif |
| png |
And the file is of a resolution of 200 x 400:
# anything below 300 pixels won't be clear enough
Then the Author sees a message informing them that the file
resolution is too low
And the file is not uploaded
```

Here, we specified a scenario where we are trying to upload a file of acceptable pixel height but not enough pixel width. This is perfectly okay; ideally, though, we would like to illustrate to our readers that uploading a file of adequate width but not enough height will also result in an error message. So, we proceed and create another Scenario, identical to the preceding one but with the difference that we swap the width and height values so that now the file is of resolution 400 x 200 (instead of 200 x 400). This works fine, but we now have introduced repetition into our Feature by having two virtually identical Scenarios that only differ in two values. Repetition is bad because it makes our Features bloated and unreadable. Luckily, the Gherkin language gives us a mechanism by which we can avoid this. We will use a Scenario Outline to avoid repeating Scenarios that use the same steps but with different parameter values:

```
Scenario Outline: Resolution too low
Given the user is logged in as an Author
And the Author goes to their Profile page
And the Author chooses to upload a picture
When the Author selects an image file from their computer
And the file is of type:
| file-type |
| jpg |
| gif |
| png |

And the file is of a resolution <width> pixels by <height>
pixels
# anything below 300 pixels won't be clear enough
Then the Author sees a message informing them that the file
resolution is too low
```

```
And the file is not uploaded


Examples:
  | width | height |
  | 200| 300 |
  | 300| 200 |
  | 299| 301 |
  | 299| 299|
```

Let's examine what we just did:

- We started our `Scenario` with the `Scenario Outline` keyword, instead of the `Scenario` keyword. This tells our readers (and also any BDD tools such as Cucumber) that this isn't a single scenario but a multi-value scenario.

- At the end of our `Scenario`, we defined an `Examples` table, with appropriate headers (width and height). We then defined a combination of different values of width and height that will incur a *failure to upload* outcome.

- In our steps, we used parameters delimited with `<>`, which reference the headers in the `Examples` table.

What that means, in practical terms, is that we compressed multiple `Scenarios` into one. Cucumber, JBehave, and so on will run this `Scenario` multiple times, once for each data row in the `Examples` table. In our specific case, that would be four times, as our `Examples` table has four data rows. Each time a `Scenario` is run, the parameters in our steps will be substituted with the values in the appropriate data row. `Scenario Outlines` are semantically and practically different to Data Tables. Let's re-iterate their difference.

Scenario Outlines versus Data Tables

`Scenario Outlines` are all about iteration and parameterization. They help us specify Scenarios that must be repeated multiple times, each time with different parameterized values.

As a rule of thumb, `Scenario Outlines` should be used where we need to illustrate system behavior for a variety of input or output data. They let our readers know that a system behavior (in other words, `Scenario`) applies within the parameters we specify and the values that these parameters may take are denoted in the `Examples` table. When we specify image resolution values in an `Examples` table, as we did previously, we are telling our readers that they should run that `Scenario` multiple times, each time with a new resolution value combination. `Scenario Outlines` apply to and affect the *entire* scenario.

`Data Tables`, on the other hand, should be used where we want to exemplify data options or constraints for specific steps in a `Scenario`. So, when we specify the permitted file types in a `Data Table`, we are telling our readers that our `Scenario` will work, as long as they use one of the file types we specify. `Data Tables` apply to and affect only specific steps.

`Scenario Outlines` and `Data Tables` are semantical constructs provided by the Gherkin language, which allows us to avoid the repetition and duplication of steps. There is yet another way to avoid duplication.

Avoiding step repetition with Backgrounds

Another way to avoid repetition in our `Scenarios` is to use a **Background**. A `Background` is simply an abstraction of steps that are duplicated across multiple `Scenarios`. In our example Feature in the previous section, every single `Scenario` begins with the same steps:

```
Given the user is logged in as an Author
And the Author goes to their Profile page
And the Author chooses to upload a picture
```

We can abstract these steps in a `Background`, so as to avoid repeating them in all our `Scenarios`:

```
Background:
Given the user is logged in as an Author
And the Author goes to their Profile page
And the Author chooses to upload a picture
```

Backgrounds are placed at the top of our Feature, before any `Scenarios`. Semantically, when we see a `Background`, we understand that the steps within it will be applied to every single `Scenario` of our Feature.

So, now that we know how to write `Features`, let's see what a complete `Feature` looks like…

Writing a fully formed Feature

In the previous sections, we examined how to fill in our Feature with Scenarios by looking at the same behavior from different angles. We also learned how to write our Feature concisely and descriptively and how to eliminate repetition, by using Data Tables, Scenario Outlines, and Backgrounds. It's time to see what our Feature will look like in its entirety:

```
Feature: Author uploads picture to profile


User Story: As an Author, I want to publish a nice picture in
my Profile, so that readers can relate to me on a human level
Impact: http://example.com/my-project/impacts-map
Screen mockups: http://example.com/my-project/mockups
Notes: Ms Smith, the CTO, really wants the Authors to upload
some nice photos of them to their profile as it helps sell more
books


Background:
Given the user is logged in as an Author
And the Author goes to their Profile page
And the Author chooses to upload a picture
And the Author selects an image file from their computer
```

Let's now write our happy path scenario. In this scenario, we are assuming that all our assumptions are correct and no constraints (file type, size, or resolution) have been violated:

```
Scenario: Successful image upload
When the selected file is of type:
  | file-type |
  | jpg |
  | gif |
  | png |
And the file is of a of a size less than  "5 " MB
And the file is of a resolution higher than  "300 " by  "300 "
pixels
And the Author uploads the file
Then the Author sees their uploaded image as their Profile
picture
```

Now let's add a scenario that describes system behavior when the file type constraint is broken:

```gherkin
Scenario: Wrong type of image
When the selected file is of type:
  | file-type |
  | svg |
  | tiff |
  | bmp |
Then the Author sees a message informing them that the file
type is not supported
And the file is not uploaded
```

We also add a Scenario that describes system behavior when the file size constraint is broken:

```gherkin
Scenario: Image too large
When the selected file is of type:
  | file-type |
  | jpg |
  | gif |
  | png |
And the file is of size greater than  "5 " MB
Then the Author sees a message informing them that the file is
too big
And the file is not uploaded
```

Finally, the following Scenario describes system behavior when the file resolution constraint is broken:

```gherkin
Scenario: Resolution too low
When the selected file is of type:
  | file-type |
  | jpg |
  | gif |
  | png |
And the file is of size less than  "5 " MB
And the file is of a resolution:
# anything below 300 pixels won't be clear enough
```

```
| width | height |
| 200| 300 |
| 300| 200 |
| 200| 200 |
Then the Author sees a message informing them that the file
resolution is too low
And the file is not uploaded
```

Our Feature has a *title* and *contextual information* (Notes, User Story, Impact Map link, and UI mockups). It details a *Happy Path Scenario* and also its inversions (remember the Rubik's cube analogy?). We say that such a Feature is a **fully formed** Feature.

So, there we have it: a nicely written Feature that covers all the main behaviors in four distinct Scenarios. Any one of our stakeholders can read this Feature and understand exactly what functionality we are delivering and how our system will behave. The extra value, though, is that our developers can take this Feature and – using a *BDD tool* such as *JBehave* or *Cucumber* – they can write some code that performs the steps specified in our Feature. That way, we can have truly executable specifications, that is, specifications that not only specify the way our system behaves but are also capable of verifying this against our delivered system code. But before we discuss executable specifications, let's examine our Feature and see what we did well and what the good practices to apply when writing Features are.

Tips for writing good Features

Features may seem easy to write but writing good Features requires focus and attention to detail. Let's take a look at one of the Scenarios we defined in the previous section, *Discovering Scenarios*:

```
Background:
Given the user is logged in as an Author
And the Author goes to their Profile page
And the Author chooses to upload a picture
And the Author selects an image file from their computer

Scenario: Successful image upload
When the selected file is of type:
| file-type |
| jpg |
| gif |
```

```
| png |
And the file is of a of a size less than  "5 " MB
And the file is of a resolution higher than  "300 " by  "300 "
pixels
And the Author uploads the file
Then the Author sees their uploaded image as their Profile
picture
```

Here are a few observations about how we wrote this `Scenario`:

- **Title**: In our Happy Path Scenario, we indicated what the **behavior** in this `Scenario` is about (*image upload*) and its **outcome** (*successful upload*). In the `Scenarios` that described unsuccessful behaviors, we described the causes of failure (*Resolution too low, Image too big*) in the titles. Our readers should be able to easily identify the happy path scenario and the causes of unsuccessful outcomes using our titles.

- **Actors**: One of the first things to do when writing `Features` is to identify the role our actor has in this particular `Feature`. In our `Background`, we clarified the actor's role (*Given the user is logged in as an Author*). This is very important as system behavior is greatly affected by the actor's role and permissions. It is crucial that throughout our scenarios, we know exactly under what guise the actor-system interactions take place. We should avoid referring to a generic user (for example, the user does something) but instead explicitly specify the Actor's role (for example, the Actor does something).

- **Steps (1)**: We use generic and abstract language to describe our steps. We avoid using technology or interface-specific language. So, we never say that the actor *clicks on the submit button to upload a picture*. We say instead that the actor *chooses to upload a picture*. We don't state that the actor *brings up the File Dialog to select an image file*. We instead say that they *select an Image File from their computer*. We do that to separate system behavior from system implementation. Today, the actor uploads a picture by clicking on a button. Tomorrow, they will be uploading the picture by selecting it from a sidebar widget. Next week, they may be uploading pictures by voice commands. The point is, the system's implementation of a behavior will change much more frequently than the system behavior itself. Always describe behaviors using generic action verbs rather than specific technical details.

- **Steps (2)**: We use imperative, present tense verbs to show behavior. We say that the author *selects an image*, not that the Author *can select an image* or *will select an image*. When we write our `Scenarios`, we imagine the actions happening before us; there is no optionality or delay involved.

- **Scenarios**: Our Scenarios are atomic. This means that each Scenario is executed completely independently from others. Conditions needed for a Scenario must be specified in their entirety in the scenario's condition (When) steps or in the Feature's Background. No scenario should rely on conditions set by a different scenario.

The Gherkin language also offers us another tool we can use to clarify and organize our Features. Let's talk about **tags**.

Using tags to label, organize, and filter our Features

Tags provide an extremely useful way to denote different contexts for our Features. They can be used to group Features together, indicate scope, filter Scenarios, and provide visual clues to our readers. Tags are just words prefixed by the @ symbol. Let's take a look at the following Feature (shortened for brevity):

```
@order
Feature: Buyer places order
@important
Scenario: Missing delivery address
   Given …


@wip @financial
Scenario: Applying discount
   Given …
```

We have applied the @order tag at the beginning of our Feature. This means that the tag applies to all the Scenarios within that Feature. If we ask a BDD tool, such as Cucumber, to run everything tagged with @order, it will execute both the Missing delivery address and Applying discount scenarios. We could apply the same tag to other Features and Scenarios too, if they were referring to order-related functionality.

We have applied the @important tag just before the Missing delivery address Scenario. This means that it applies to that Scenario only. Getting Cucumber to run @important Scenarios will only execute this one Scenario.

We have applied the @wip and @financial tags just before the Applying discount Scenario. This means that both of these tags apply to this Scenario. Cucumber will execute this Scenario when we tell it to run either the @wip or @financial tag (or both).

We can use any permutation of tags in any order we deem useful. Tools such as Cucumber allow the running of multiple tag combinations; they can even negate tags, so we could, for instance, tell Cucumber to run all Scenarios with the @important tag but omit any Scenarios with the @wip tag. In addition to these practical benefits, tags also provide visual contextual information to our Feature's readers.

By using tags and following the tips in the previous section, we will write readable and reliable executable specifications. Speaking of which, let's see exactly how our specifications, that is, our Features, become executable.

Knowing why Features are executable specifications

So far, we've created a Feature that captures our system's *Author uploads profile picture* behavior. Our Feature is the one and only source of truth for our development team. They can now take this Feature and write and deploy code that implements the behaviors specified in our Feature. But how do we know that the code that our developers will deliver actually makes the system behave as specified? Well, there's an easy way to find out: we write some **step definitions** for our Scenario steps. A step definition is simply some code that executes the behavior specified in a step. So, in our sample Feature, we have a Background that states the following:

```
Background:
Given the user is logged in as an Author
And the Author goes to their Profile page
And the Author chooses to upload a picture
And the Author selects an image file from their computer
```

We then write some code, in our programming language of choice, which sets up and runs our system and does the following:

1. Logs in a test user as an Author

2. Loads the profile page

3. Clicks the **Upload photo** button

4. Selects a file for upload from a specific folder

So, for each step in our Scenario, we have a relevant piece of code that does what the step specifies. We call this a **step definition**. Our step definitions live in our code base, but in separate files to our Features. We put our Features in files with the .feature extension, while our step definitions reside in files with an appropriate language extension, such as .rb for Ruby, .py for Python, .java for Java, and so on. If our sample feature is saved in the <project-dir>/features/author_uploads_profile_photo. feature file and we use Cucumber for Ruby to verify our specifications, then our step definitions file would be <project-dir>/features/step_definitions/ author_uploads_profile_photo.rb.

> **Tip**
> The directory structure for our feature and step definitions files is dictated by the BDD tool we use to run our executable specifications. For the purposes of this book, we shall assume a <project-dir>/features/ step_definitions structure. Feature files (.feature) go under the features directory, while step definition files (.rb, .py, .java) go under the step_definitions directory.

Let's assume we use Cucumber for Ruby (https://cucumber.io/docs/ installation/). Our author_uploads_profile_photo.rb file will contain code that looks like this:

```ruby
Given( "the user is logged in as an Author ") do
  # Some code that turns the phrase above into concrete actions
visit '/sessions/new'
    within( "#session ") do
      fill_in 'Email', with: 'author@example.com'
      fill_in 'Password', with: 'password'

end
Given( "the Author goes to their Profile page ") do
  # Some code that turns the phrase above into concrete actions
visit '/authors/profile'
end

Given( "the Author chooses to upload a picture ") do
  # Some code that turns the phrase above into concrete actions
```

```
click_button( "Upload photo ")
expect(page).to have_content 'File path'
end


Given( "the Author selects an image file from their computer ")
do
   # Some code that turns the phrase above into concrete actions
attach_file('photo-file', 'path/to/myphoto.png)
end
```

You may have noticed that the Scenario steps in our Feature file are matched in our step definition file. In fact, this is how BDD tools, such as Cucumber, manage to run our executable specifications: they read the steps in the Feature files and then they look for matching steps in our step definitions files and execute the relevant code. This is illustrated in the following diagram:

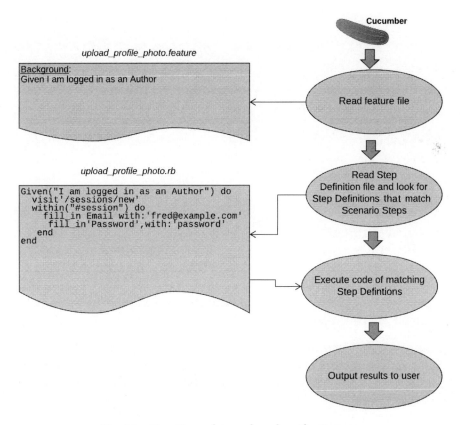

Fig. 3.2 – How Cucumber reads and verifies Features

As the preceding figure shows, Cucumber will read our Feature file and parse *I am logged in as an Author* as a `Scenario` step. It will then scan our step definitions files for a step definition that matches the text of the step. When it finds it, it will execute the Ruby code in the matching step definition. As we can also see in the preceding figure, all the step definition does for that step is go to the login page and enter a valid username and password. If our system behaves the way we described in our `Scenarios`, then the step definition code will run flawlessly. If not, the code will fail, and Cucumber will report the errors in a readable format. If we tell Cucumber to run our `Feature`, its output will look like this:

```
➜ cucumber -f summary features/profile_photo_upload.feature
Author uploads picture to profile
  Successful image upload ✓
  Wrong type of image ✓
  Image too large ✓
  Resolution too low ✓
4 scenarios (4 passed)
32 steps (32 passed)
0m0.025s
```

Fig. 3.3 – Output for our Feature

As you can see, Cucumber tells us exactly how many `Scenarios` and steps were ran successfully. By running a BDD tool such as Cucumber regularly, we can get an accurate picture of our development progress at any given time. This book is not intended to make you a Cucumber (or JBehave or Behat) expert. Instead, we want you to learn how to leverage BDD and how to write solid, verifiable `Features`. Actually, that is the topic of the next chapter, so stay tuned.

Summary

In this chapter, we learned how to write complete and clear `Features`. **Features** are at the heart of requirements management; they are our system's specifications, and they drive our whole development effort. This is why it is so important to be able to write accurate `Features` that are easy to read, clearly describe our system's behavior, and are easy to verify. By now, you should be armed with the knowledge needed to write a `Feature` correctly, completely, and accurately.

However, we haven't finished with `Features` just yet. In the next chapter, you will learn how to craft `Features` – that is, how to create `Features` that are not only written correctly but are also high-quality, consistent, and stable. So, read on to become a true `Feature` craftsperson.

Further reading

- Matt Wynne, Aslak Hellesoy – *The Cucumber Book: Behaviour-Driven Development for Testers and Developers, The Pragmatic Programmers, 2nd Edition*, ISBN-13: 978-1680502381

- Wayne Ye – *Instant Cucumber BDD How-To*, Packt Publishing, ISBN-13: 978-1782163480

4

Crafting Features Using Principles and Patterns

In the previous chapter, we learned how to write `Features` correctly. In this chapter, we will take it one step further. We will learn how to craft our `Features`. Creating something can be done by following an instruction set. Crafting something is different. It takes skill, deep knowledge of the materials and domain we're working with, and intuition derived from trial and error. In this chapter, we'll be crafting Features by applying principles and patterns in order to write high-quality, maintainable, and verifiable `Features`. In particular, we will cover the following:

- **Behavior-Driven Development (BDD)** principles
- Discerning patterns in our `Features`
- Patterns to avoid

After reading this chapter, you will be confident that you can write solid, future-proof `Features` by using the right mental models and discerning which patterns to apply and which to avoid.

Applying the BDD principles

The best way to ensure that we write good Features is to adhere to certain principles that will help us avoid mistakes and increase the quality of our Features. In this section, we will examine the four major mental models to help us write concise, descriptive, and well-scoped Features. Let's start at understanding that BDD is not about testing.

BDD isn't testing

BDD is about collaboration and shared understanding. By writing our features using a structured and ubiquitous language that can be understood by all stakeholders, we provide clarity and transparency. We allow and invite non-technical stakeholders to get involved in specifying our system's behavior. We make sure we all sing from the same hymn sheet, and that hymn sheet is our features, that is, our specifications. Yes, we also provide executable step definitions so that we can verify that our delivered code works as described in our features. But do not make the mistake of confusing this with testing. If you approach BDD with a *testing* mentality, you will start thinking as a tester, not as an actor in a specific feature. Having a testing mentality will, inevitably, lead to adding implementation details into your scenarios, thinking about 100% coverage and other such practices that will make your features unreadable and unusable. We will cover the effects of such bad practices later on when we look at anti-patterns.

The 80-20 rule

Also known as the **Pareto principle**, this is a probabilistic distribution rule originally applied to wealth distribution. According to the original application of the rule, 80% of the wealth of a society is held by 20% of its population. It was subsequently found that this rule also applies to other areas of human and natural activity. For instance, 80% of your company's revenue will be generated by 20% of your customers, 80% of your system's errors will be caused by 20% of your system's bugs, as Microsoft already discovered, (https://www.crn.com/news/security/18821726/microsofts-ceo-80-20-rule-applies-to-bugs-not-just-features.htm), and so on.

This rule applies to our features too. 80% of a feature's transpired behavior will be reflected in 20% of our scenarios. What does this mean? It means that when our feature is in actual use, chances are that 20% of the scenarios we have come up with will be invoked 80% of the time. The implication is that we shouldn't try to cover every eventuality with a scenario. In our sample *Author uploads profile picture* feature, we identified four basic behaviors and created four scenarios:

1. Successful image upload
2. Wrong type of image

3.   Image too large

4.   Resolution too low

With these scenarios, we've covered the most likely behaviors. When our actor tries to upload a file, it is almost certain that one of these behaviors will come into effect. By reading the feature and its scenarios, our stakeholder knows exactly how our system will behave 99% of the time when an author tries to upload a profile picture.

You may ask, "*But what if the internet connection is very slow and the picture takes a long time to upload? Shouldn't we have a Scenario for this eventuality?*" Yes, that may happen. But what are the chances of it happening? We've already prevented large files from being uploaded. If your internet takes a long time to upload a few MBs, then you have bigger problems to worry about than simply uploading your profile picture. Focus on the behaviors that are likely to occur instead of the behaviors that may occur. Focus on the behaviors that matter to stakeholders, not the ones that matter to you. Look out for behaviors that fall within your sphere of control, not outside it. Look out for probable scenarios instead of possible scenarios. 20% of the scenarios we can think of will be invoked 80% of the time. Don't worry about exceptional or unique circumstances.

System behavior is not system implementation

When we write our features, we are specifying behavior. We are saying this:

> *"As the Actor involved in this Feature and given certain conditions, when some actions occur, then I expect a specific outcome. I don't care about how this outcome came to be or what technologies this outcome utilizes. I may not even care about what this outcome looks like. As long the expected outcome happens, I am happy."*

Feature writers sometimes tend to add statements to scenarios such as "*Then the message is pushed to a queue*" or "*And a pop-up dialog with a warning icon is displayed.*" The truth is, the actor who is directly involved in this behavior couldn't care less about the message getting in a queue, a stack, or on a conveyor belt, for that matter. They just want the message successfully delivered. Similarly, most people who use computers don't really care about messages popping up with a yellow warning mark next to them. They care about having information conveyed to them in a clear, unambiguous manner. Whether this information is presented in a pop-up dialog with rounded edges or a flash message across their screen is not of great importance to them. The people using the system care about the behavior much more than the implementation of that behavior.

> **Tip**
>
> Most actors tend to care about the **What**, **Where**, and **When** of their
> interactions with the system, not the **How**. They want to know what the system
> does, when it does it, where it does it, and with what they need to respond.
> How the system does what it does is of little interest to them.

Our specifications describe our system's behavior from the actors' point of view. Our
executable step definitions need to know about the implementation of this behavior.
Our features are only concerned with the behavior itself.

> **Important note:**
>
> An exception to the preceding rule is where implementation does affect
> behavior. This is most notable in accessibility-related features. For instance,
> if we implement some behavior with mouse or gesture-only actions, then we
> are withholding this behavior from system users who don't use a mouse or a
> touchpad. If we implement displaying a message in certain color hues, then we
> may be affecting our system's behavior with respect to color-blind users. In such
> cases, it may be wise to add the implementation details in our scenario steps.

Wearing different hats

Within an organization, we all have specific roles and job titles. We are software engineers,
architects, project managers, testers, and so on. We are used to seeing things from the
perspective of our assigned role. We may all look at the same problem, but we each
see different things. What is important to a software engineer will not have the same
importance to an end user, for instance. To be able to write features correctly, we need to
overcome this mental hurdle. When we're thinking about a feature, we must be able to
discard our usual hat and wear the same hat as the actor involved in that feature. Only
then will we be able to see what is important to that actor and be able to capture these
important things in the Feature.

Discerning patterns in our features

Feature patterns are general, repeatable outlines or models of the way `Feature` is
written or what it represents. Because patterns are repeated, we have learned to know
the implications of applying (or not applying) specific patterns. Being able to discern
patterns in our features means that we can anticipate potential problems and pre-empt
them. It also means that we can choose to apply a pattern that is known to be beneficial, if
conditions allow it. Let's examine the main feature patterns.

The CRUD Features pattern

CRUD stands for **C**reate, **R**ead, **U**pdate, **D**elete. It's a very common term in software engineering, used to denote generic read/write operations or behaviors. Let's imagine that we are developing a blogging system. We have outlined our impact map, as illustrated in the following figure:

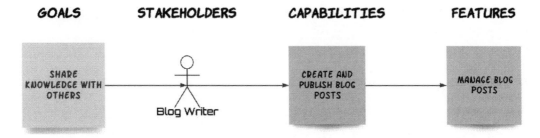

Fig. 4.1 – A CRUD Feature

Our main capability is **CREATE AND PUBLISH BLOG POSTS**. This clearly involves more than just creating a post and making it available to our users. Our blog writers will also need to make changes to their post, re-publish it, and even delete it, if the circumstances demand.

So, we decide that we'll deliver the capability by implementing a **MANAGE BLOG POSTS** feature. Our feature will have scenarios for creating, updating, and deleting a blog post. At first sight, this looks reasonable. However, let's think this through: we'll need to have three `Happy Path Scenarios`, one for each of our create, update, delete behaviors. We'll also have at least three more failure scenarios, one for each of these behaviors. We'll probably need to have a separate *Publish post* scenario to illustrate what happens after the post is created. The *Edit* behavior will also very likely behave differently depending on whether the edit occurs for a published or unpublished post. If you're keeping count, we have nine scenarios so far. We will also need to define the behavior when we try to publish a post with a title that belongs to another published post. Also, the behavior of deleting a post that is currently being read by other users will have to be captured. That's 11 scenarios and counting.

To cut a long story short, accumulating CRUD behaviors in the same feature can (and does) lead to large, convoluted Features that are difficult to read and understand. A much better practice is to separate our CRUD feature into distinct features for each CRUD behavior, as shown in the following diagram:

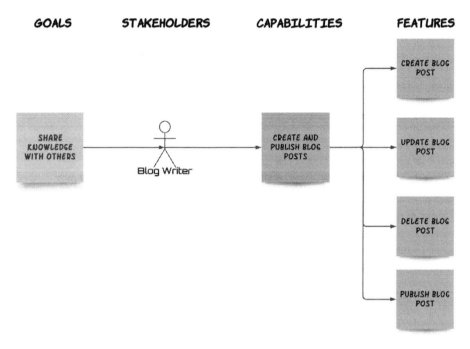

Fig. 4.2 – CRUD Feature simplified

By decomposing our CRUD behaviors, instead of one large, unreadable feature, we have four concise features with only a few scenarios each, which are far easier for our stakeholders to read and for us to manage.

The composite features pattern

Let's imagine that, while analyzing requirements for our blogging platform, we have created a *Create User Profile* feature. It involves the user writing a short biography (bio), adding a tagline, and uploading a photo, as depicted in the following mock-up provided by our stakeholders:

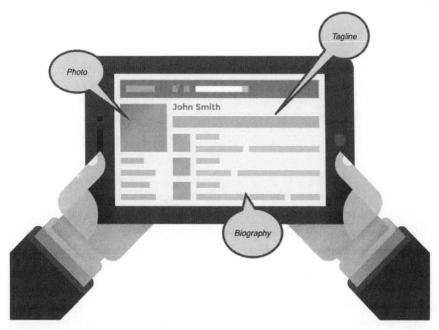

Fig. 4.3 – Create profile mock-up screen

We can readily identify at least three `Happy Path Scenarios` for our feature, as per the areas of required functionality:

- `Scenario`: Successfully write biography
- `Scenario`: Successfully write tagline
- `Scenario`: Successfully upload photo

Much as we described in the *CRUD Features* pattern, this can quickly escalate to dozens of scenarios, when we take into account different scenarios for each area of functionality (biography, photo, tagline). To solve the problem, we apply the same solution we did to the *CRUD Features* pattern: we break down the complex functionality into its sub-functionalities. So, we're going to replace the big, composite *Create Profile* feature with three new, smaller features:

- Write biography
- Set tagline
- Upload profile photo

By doing so, we have created features that are more readable and easily managed, while also ensuring that each feature focuses on very specific behaviors.

> **Important information**
>
> Composites and CRUD are sibling patterns. The main difference is that CRUD features group together dissimilar operations (create, update, and delete) within the same area of functionality (blog posts), while composite features group together similar operations within dissimilar sub-areas of functionality (biography, tags, and photo). Often, features will be composite and CRUD at the same time. In such cases, we need to break down the composite parts first. This will leave us with a set of new, smaller CRUD features for distinct functionality areas. Then, for each new feature, we will break down its CRUD operations into further new features, one for each CRUD operation in that distinct area.

The feature interpolation pattern

In *Chapter 2, Impact Mapping and Behavior-Driven Development*, we discussed **Non-Functional Requirements** (**NFRs**) and explained how we can model them in the same way as functional requirements, using the standard **Goal-Capability-Feature Impact Map** model. Many NFRs are cross-cutting, in that they affect a number of other features in our system. Such requirements may be represented as separate capabilities and features, or they can be interpolated within other features. Let's look at the example of the blogging system from the previous section, *CRUD Features*. After talking with the relevant stakeholders, we write a *Create Blog Post* feature like this:

```
Feature: Blog writer creates post


User Story: As a Writer, when I have some information worth
sharing with my peers, I want to make it available to them, so
that my peers are helped and my reputation increases
Impact: http://example.com/my-project-impacts-map


Background:
Given the user is logged in as a Writer
And the Writer goes to their MyPosts page


Scenario: Successful post creation
When the Writer chooses to create a post
And the Writer writes a title "iPhone SE review" for the post
```

```
And the Writer writes a body for the post
And the Writer chooses to save the post
Then the MyPosts page lists a post titled 'iPhone SE review'
```

Our marketing director now comes in and tells us that, according to their research, many users want to use our blogging system on all of their devices, such as desktop computers, laptops, tablets, and cellphones. Consequently, we need to provide the functionality for them to create blog posts from any device they are using. There are two ways we can model this requirement:

- **Option 1**: We create a specific capability, for example, using the system on different devices and deriving some features. In the example depicted in the following figure, we have our actor wanting to create, read, and rate blog posts on a variety of devices:

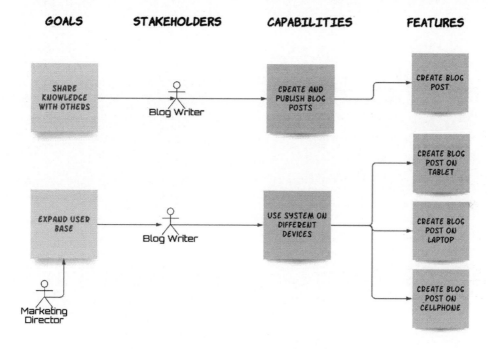

Fig. 4.4 – New Capability and Features for NFR

The problem with this approach should be obvious simply by looking at this impact map: duplication. We have already created the *blog-creation* feature when we analyzed the *Create and Publish Blog Posts* capability. The only difference between the *Create Blog Post* and *Create Blog Post on Tablet* features would be that the latter would have an extra scenario step, such as *Given I am using an iPad*, to reflect the multi-device capability we need to support. Clearly, this approach is wasteful and superfluous. Fear not, though; we can model our new requirement using a different approach, as follows.

- **Option 2**: We interpolate the new behavior into the existing *Create Blog Post* feature. This would be done simply by adding some extra conditional steps to reflect our multi-device constraint:

```
Feature: Blog writer creates post

User Story: As a Writer, when I have some information
worth sharing with my peers, I want to make it available
to them, so that my peers are helped and my reputation
increases

Impact: http://example.com/my-project-impacts-map


Background:
Given the user is logged in as a Writer

### new step below:
And the Writer is using a:
| device |
| MacBook |
| Windows laptop |
| iPhone |
| Android phone |
| Android tablet |
| iPad |


And the Writer goes to their MyPosts page


Scenario: Successful post creation
When the Writer chooses to create a post
And the Writer writes a title "iPhone SE review" for the
post
And the Writer writes a body for the post
And the Writer chooses to save the post
Then the MyPosts page lists a post titled 'iPhone SE
review'
```

As you can see, the only difference between the original feature and the re-written feature is that we added a new `Background` step with a data table to account for the different devices the Writer can create a blog post on. Our impact map is also greatly simplified, as illustrated in the following figure:

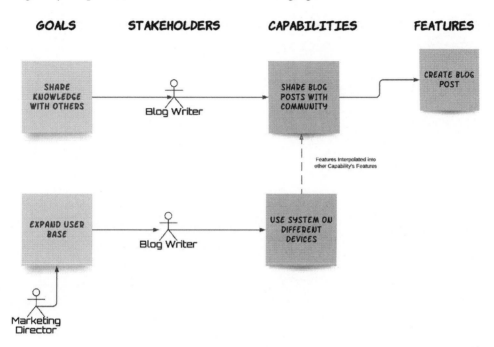

Fig. 4.5 – Interpolated Features

Interpolating features is a very effective way to model NFRs. By identifying the capability suggested by the NFR (and its associated stakeholders and goals), we captured the requirement and assessed its impact. At the same time, we didn't duplicate effort by creating new features and we didn't pollute our requirements model unnecessarily.

Now that we know which patterns help us improve our features, let's take a look at which patterns hinder them.

Patterns to avoid

Anti-patterns are patterns that are known to produce adverse effects, such as making features too large, difficult to understand, or hard to verify. These patterns are to be spotted early and avoided. This section presents some of the most common anti-patterns found in the wild.

Anti-pattern – thinking like developers

Let's look at a `Scenario` written for our system's *Search for Books* feature:

```
Given I am a Book Reviewer
When I go to 'http://example.com/search'
And I click on the Search button
And I see a search text box with the id #search_books
And I enter "adams + galaxy"
Then I'm redirected to the results page
And I see the 'The Hitchhiker's Guide to the Galaxy' by Douglas
Adams
```

Here, we can easily tell that this scenario was written by a software developer or some other technical person, simply by looking at the amount of technical details described. *Step 2* has a URL in it. *Step 3* specifies an HTML element (button). *Step 4* refers to a CSS ID. *Step 5* specifies the plus operator. *Step 6* mentions a redirection. The reason that this is problematic is that such technical details – while being obviously valuable to a software developer or tester – are totally irrelevant to the actor who'll be exercising this scenario. Our Book Reviewer doesn't care much about the URL they visit or the type and ID of HTML element they interact with, and they probably don't even know what a re-direction is.

> **Tip**
> Neglecting the *Wearing Different Hats* principle is the main cause of the thinking-like-developers anti-pattern.

Let's re-write this scenario from the Book Reviewer's perspective:

```
Given I am a Book Reviewer
When I go to the search page
And I search for 'adams' and 'galaxy'
Then I see 'The Hitchhiker's Guide to the Galaxy' by Douglas
Adams
```

It's really that simple. This is all the Book Reviewer cares about when searching. Let's not confuse our readers with irrelevant technical details.

Anti-pattern – incidental details

Let's look at a `Scenario` for our user login behavior:

```
Given I am a Book Reviewer
When I go to the login page
And I enter 'Fred' as the username
And I enter 'mypassword' as the password
Then I see a message:
"""
Welcome Fred. Happy reading!
"""
```

At first sight, nothing seems wrong with this scenario – that is, until we start thinking about the value each step adds to the Book Reviewer. Do they really need to know about a specific username or password? Also, what would happen if our Book Reviewer saw a message that said, "*Hello Fred*" instead of, "*Welcome, Fred. Happy reading!*"? I think it is safe to assume they wouldn't really mind either way.

> **Tip**
> In our scenarios, we only capture the behavior and details that are important to the actor involved. We don't capture specifics unless they reflect some essential business rule or constraint. Ignoring the *system behavior is not system implementation* principle will often cause this anti-pattern.

So, let's re-write our `Scenario` in a way that captures what our Book Reviewer really cares about:

```
Given I am a Book Reviewer
When I go to the login page
And I enter a valid username and password
Then I see a welcome message
```

By removing incidental details, we make our scenario not only more readable but also more resistant to change. The text of the welcome message and specific credentials will change often. The behavior depicted in our scenario, however, is much more likely to remain the same.

Anti-pattern – scenario flooding

In this anti-pattern, our Feature is flooded with dozens of scenarios. This makes our feature difficult to read, as most people find it difficult to read beyond a handful of scenarios in a feature. It can also make it longer to write step definitions (verification code) for that many scenarios. Too many scenarios indicates an overlapping of different functionalities in the same feature, or a pre-occupation with edge-case behaviors. The usual causes of this anti-pattern are the following:

1. Ignoring the *BDD isn't about testing* principle. People who think of writing Features as a way of testing the system will usually go for 100% test coverage, and that leads to a huge number of scenarios, most of which aren't likely to be exercised often.

2. Ignoring the *80-20 rule* principle. People will often write down Scenario simply because they can think of it, rather than because it helps illustrate a specific behavior. We write scenarios to show our stakeholders how the system will behave under most working conditions, not to demonstrate how many edge cases we can think of.

3. The feature is a CRUD or composite feature (see the *The CRUD Features pattern* section) that hasn't been simplified.

4. The feature is actually a capability. Capabilities are much more coarsely grained and treating them as Features will produce a plethora of scenarios. If unsure, check *Chapter 3, Writing Fantastic Features with the Gherkin Language*, specifically the *Capabilities versus Features* section.

Having too many scenarios in our feature not only deters people from reading it but also makes it harder (and longer) to implement. Ideally, features should be implemented within 2 working weeks, which is the minimum duration of a Scrum sprint, as we'll discover in *Chapter 7, Feature-First Development*, specifically the *Working with Scrum* section. As a rule of thumb, more than nine scenarios in a feature should be a cause for concern and should prompt a re-evaluation of that Feature.

Anti-pattern – vague outcomes

Let's imagine we have just written the following Feature:

```
Given I am a Blog Author
And I am editing my blog post
When I change the existing title to a new title
And I save the changes
Then my post title has been updated
```

This makes perfect sense to us. After all, we know exactly how the system is supposed to work. But let's consider how this looks like from someone else's point of view. Someone who doesn't know what *post title has been updated* means. Does it mean that they can now see the new title on the current page? Do they need to go to a different page to see the updated title? That last step is just too vague to answer those questions. Even more importantly, the developer who writes the step definitions, that is, the code that verifies this step, may not know how to verify it. Ignorance breeds assumptions. So, they may just go and write some code that checks that the new title has been updated in the system database while ignoring the UI. This may lead to a disastrous situation where the scenario will be successfully verified when we run the step definitions, but the system will not behave as the user expects. The solution to this conundrum is to be specific about our scenario outcomes. Let's re-write our `Scenario` as follows:

```
Given I am a Blog Author
And I am editing my blog post
When I change the existing title to a new title
And I save the changes
Then I see a listing of my blog posts
And I see that my edited blog post now has a new title
```

We now have a specific outcome that leaves little room for ambiguity or misunderstanding. But we can make this even clearer:

```
Given I am a Blog Author
And I have a blog post titled 'Gone with the wind'
And I am editing this blog post
When I change the post title to 'Casablanca'
And I save the changes
Then I see a listing of my blog posts
And I see one of my blogs is titled 'Casablanca'
And none of my blogs is titled 'Gone with the wind'
```

We are now using specific examples to convey the full impact of the behavior we are describing in a clear, understandable manner.

> **Tip**
> Never neglect the *Wearing Different Hats* principle, as it is the main cause of the vague outcomes anti-pattern.

Anti-pattern – compound steps

Compound steps are **Scenario steps** that blend in more than one action within a single step. Let's look at this example of a compound step:

```
When I enable the 'per diem' and 'travel allowance' options
```

Now let's re-write it as two separate steps:

```
When I enable the 'per diem' option
And I enable the 'travel allowance' option
```

Having two separate steps makes our behavior much more obvious, as we are clarifying that we are referring to two distinct actions. It also helps implement step definitions as we are clearly delineating different parts of the UI we need to code against when verifying those steps.

Sometimes, compound steps are subtle and hard to detect, as here:

```
When I add a unique email
```

Here we have a step that looks like it comprises a single action. This is an illusion, though. When we add a unique email, in reality, we do two things:

1. We come up with an email name.
2. We check that the email is not taken by anyone else in our domain or organization; that is, we check whether it's a unique email.

The person who writes the step definition for this will also have to perform these two actions in order to verify this behavior. So, let's just help them out and write our step as follows:

```
When I add an email
And that email is unique
```

Not only did we make it easier to write step definitions, we opened the path to discover new scenarios, such as what happens when the email we add is not unique. Much better all around!

Summary

In this chapter, we learned how to apply good practices in order to produce high-quality `Features`. Features are at the heart of requirements management: they are our system's specifications, and they drive our whole development effort. This is why it is so important to be able to write non-brittle `Features` that are easy to read, fully describe our system's behavior, and are easy to verify. By now, you should be armed with the knowledge needed to write a `Feature` correctly, accurately, and legibly, and be able to futureproof it by knowing which principles to follow and which patterns to apply or to avoid.

So far, we have learned what a requirements model is, which entities constitute this model (goals, stakeholders, capabilities, and features), and how to create this model and correctly define and describe our entities. In the next chapter, we will take an in-depth look at how to analyze requirements in order to identify, define, and create our requirements model. So, put your analytical hat on and get ready to learn some interesting new methods and techniques.

5
Discovering and Analyzing Requirements

In the previous three chapters, we learned how to create goals, stakeholders, capabilities, and features, how to write these correctly, and how to use them to create a requirements model, represented as an impact map. Still, there is a very important part of the modeling process that we haven't touched upon in much detail: how to draw the requirements out of our stakeholders and extract well-defined requirement entities from these requirements. This is what we intend to examine in this chapter. Specifically, we will cover the following:

- The lost art of requirements elicitation
- Preparing for requirements analysis
- Analyzing requirements
- Having a structured conversation
- **Decompose, Derive, Discover (D3)**
- Business process mapping

By the end of the chapter, you will know why requirements elicitation is so important yet so casually handled in today's agile world. You will also have learned about a couple of essential artifacts that will help you with requirements elicitation. Finally, you will be aware of three effective techniques for discovering, analyzing, and mapping requirements to an impact map.

The lost art of requirements elicitation

Agile methods have, rightly so, become the standard way of creating and delivering software systems. Most agile frameworks and methodologies do not prescribe any way of capturing requirements and translating them into specifications. To fill this gap, most analysts and developers resort to using user stories as the starting point for the analysis and development process. As alluded to in previous chapters, user stories are usually too wide in scope and context to serve a useful purpose without a huge amount of context-filtering and descoping. This leads to what is known as **user-story hell**, where our product backlog consists of dozens of different stories, describing everything from non-acting stakeholders' wishes to technical constraints. Such backlogs are extremely difficult to manage or prioritize.

So, when a stakeholder tells us they want something from our system, we have two options.

The **first option** is that we create a user story, usually in the template of *As a <stakeholder>, I want <some functionality>, so that <some benefit>*. We then go and have a conversation with the stakeholder about how this functionality should work, write down a narrative, capture some business rules or constraints, and write some acceptance criteria. We then put these stories on the backlog for everyone to read.

Sounds good right? Well, it isn't. Here's why:

- No-one, apart from the story creator, knows where the story came from. No-one knows why this story exists, what business goal it's serving, whether there are other, better ways to achieve that business goal, whether that business goal is a valid one, or even whether this story duplicates or conflicts with another story. All we have is a user story; just a post-it note, sitting there among dozens of other post-it notes.

- To implement the functionality in the story, we first need to make some sense out of it. This often involves splitting the story into smaller stories, perhaps pulling some acceptance criteria out as separate stories. If the story is too big to be delivered as a single unit, we may call it an **epic**. We sometimes create new user stories to capture technical constraints or business rules. All these are arbitrary and subjective ways of dealing with the chaos of user stories. They leave behind a jumbled mess of multi-level, multi-context stories that are very difficult to work with.

The **second option** is to analyze the requirement, identify and capture the requirement entities it encapsulates, and model these in a structured, hierarchical, and highly legible impact map.

This approach has some distinct advantages:

- We can identify stakeholder goals and validate the requirement against them.
- We can easily identify conflicting or duplicating functionalities.
- We can trace features (functionalities) to capabilities to stakeholders and goals.
- We can easily see, organize, and prioritize our backlog.

As illustrated in the following figure, a requirements model enables us to easily understand what the requirements are, as well as their scope and context. It also provides visual traceability between the different entities, so that anyone working on even the smallest task to implement a feature can see exactly the overall context (the big picture) of what they are working on:

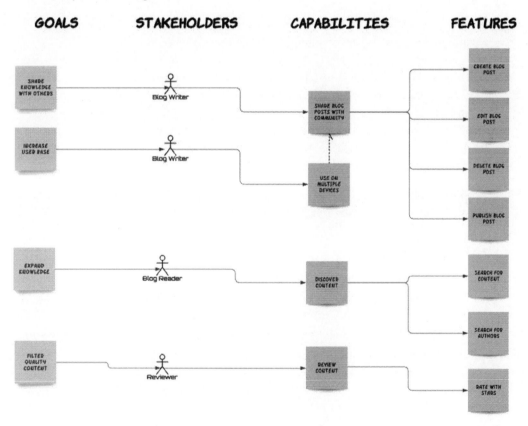

Fig. 5.1 – Example of a requirements model

Compare the preceding diagram of a structured, contextualized, and hierarchical requirements model to the stack of user stories we would have had if we chose the first option. A thorough analysis of the requirements will result in this informative and manageable model, which will be the basis for our system development effort. In this chapter, we will learn how to analyze requirements and identify and capture the requirement entities they encapsulate. It is the final skill that is needed in order to be able to fulfill the requirements and specifications and do so in a consistent, efficient, and reliable manner.

Preparing for requirements analysis

Before we start eliciting and modeling requirements, it is very important that we do the following:

- Understand who uses and/or influences our system, that is, the stakeholders. It is absolutely crucial that we know who will be interacting with our system before we try to understand what they want to achieve by using our system.

- Ensure that we use a common language with our stakeholders. The usage of different semantics and ambiguous terms can be catastrophic when eliciting requirements. I once got through the best part of a 1-hour meeting before realizing that three of us in the room were using the term **session** in totally different ways: my colleague – a network engineer – meant a TCP session, I was talking about an HTTP (browser) session, while our client – a stockbroker – was referring to a trading session! Ridiculous as it may sound, such mix-ups and ambiguities are all too common when people from different knowledge domains come together.

To accomplish these pre-requisites, we need to create two artifacts: a stakeholder model and a glossary. Let's examine them in the subsequent sections.

Stakeholder model

In *Chapter 1*, *The Requirements Domain*, we discussed how to identify stakeholders and categorize actors. Knowing which stakeholders are involved in our system is essential if we want to discover and correctly model requirements. Let's imagine that we are building a university college learning management system. A complete stakeholder model would look something like this:

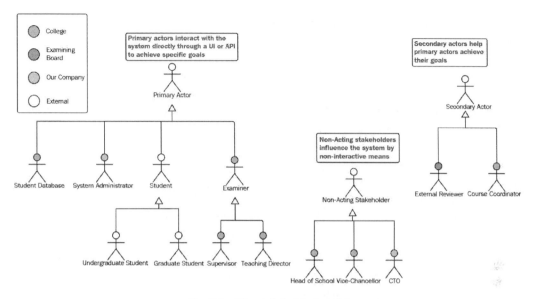

Fig. 5.2 – The stakeholder model

What the stakeholder model achieves is the following:

- **Identification of the primary actors, secondary actors, and non-acting stakeholders**: This helps us to understand who triggers our system behavior and how they affect the system. If we receive any requirements from a stakeholder who is not modeled here, we need to ask ourselves (and others) whether that stakeholder has a good reason to want to influence our system. If the answer is yes, we add the stakeholder to our model and examine their requirements. The model allows us to know who influences our system and how, at a single glance.

- **Allows us to generalize actors**: Generalizing actors allows us to capture system behavior that may vary under different conditions. For instance, we are expecting our students to interact with our system. But these interactions will be slightly different depending on whether the student is an undergraduate or graduate student. Our supervisor and teaching director expect certain functionalities allowed to them by the system and certain system behaviors. But, sometimes, either of these actors may need to act like an examiner. In this case, they would expect different functionalities and system behaviors.

- It describes stakeholders' roles and responsibilities. A good model will have annotations or comments for most stakeholders. For instance, the annotation for the supervisor will be something like *A teaching staff member who is responsible for maintaining the academic progress and well-being of specific students.*

- It depicts the organizational affiliations of the stakeholders. This can be very useful. For example, knowing that the system administrator will be a member of your team will make a considerable difference to how and when you elicit their requirements.

Another thing of note is that our actors are not always human ones. Any external system or API we need to interact with is itself an actor. For example, our college system will need to get and send data to the university's student database. The student database system is an actor because it will influence our system's behavior by interacting with it.

> **Tip**
> Avoid using vague and generic actors. Specifically, avoid using the *user* actor. It is a catch-all term that only creates confusion and ambiguity and will hinder your requirements elicitation process.

The stakeholder model is a constantly evolving artifact. It starts small and then it grows as our understanding increases. Once we've created our stakeholder model, we need to strive to have conversations with each actor representative, which is someone who has the role and responsibilities of the actor in question and can answer our questions.

Discovering stakeholders

Anyone who will be interacting with our system or influencing its behavior in any other way is a stakeholder. Looking at the email distribution list for project meetings is a sure-fire way of discovering stakeholders. We may also discover stakeholders by asking the following questions:

- Who (or what) needs information from the system?
- Who (or what) does the system need information from?
- Who maintains the system?
- Who is going to be affected if the system is not delivered?

Another way to discover stakeholders is to look at our client's business process diagrams. We'll talk more about this technique further on in this chapter.

Glossary

Glossary is a Greek-derived word that literally means *a book of language*. This is very apt, as this is exactly what we want to have while talking to our stakeholders. A glossary is just a table with two columns. The first column is the term, word, or phrase we are defining, and the second column displays its disambiguated meaning. There are two concepts to consider when clarifying meaning:

- **Polysemy** occurs when the same word has different meanings in different contexts. The previously mentioned *session* means different things in the web development world, the networking and infrastructure world, and the stock-brokering world. The word *mole* means different things depending on whether you're talking about your garden or your face. The phrase *drawing a gun* means something different to a graphics designer than to a bank robber.

- **Synonymizing** is the usage of different words to convey the same meaning based on different contexts. Within the same knowledge domain, we may have the same action represented by different words or phrases depending on the system actor or the system state.

For instance, in our everyday life, we usually say that we *upload* a document to a website. However, I have worked on a publishing system where its users did not *upload* documents to the website, but **submitted** documents instead. In addition, *submitted* was only used when it was the students who uploaded the document. A reviewer could then review and annotate the document before uploading it to a different system for final review, and that upload was called **processing** because it was done by the reviewer and it meant the document was now ready for publication. Finally, an editor would upload the document to yet another publishing system. That upload was called **publishing**. So, here we have this common, singular action that you and I would call *uploading* being called *submitting*, *processing*, or *publishing* depending on who was doing it and the state of the document at that point. Using the wrong term at the wrong time or for the wrong actor will cause confusion.

A glossary will look something like this:

Term	Definition
UI	User Interface
API	Application Programming Interface
Stakeholder	Someone or something that derives value, benefits from or exerts influence on the system.
Actor	Someone or something that interacts with the system through a UI, API or other means. All actors are stakeholders but a stakeholder isn't necessarily an actor.
Capability	A system ability that enables a stakeholder to achieve a business goal. capabilities provide a high-level view of *what the system does*, not *how* it does it.
Feature	A system functionality that helps deliver a capability. Features describe the system behaviour, not its design or architecture, i.e. they describe *how the system works* from the actors' perspective. Features are described in business domain terminology and are structured in the form of a descriptive user-story and a number of acceptance criteria (*Scenarios*).
Session	A timed interaction between Supervisor and Student that aims to transfer knowledge, answer questions and clarify issues. Sessions are conducted between a Supervisor and one or a few (no more than 4) Students.
Q&A	A timed interaction between one or more Supervisors and many Students which is conducted in a structured way by having a Student asking a question, followed by a Supervisor providing an answer.

Fig. 5.3 – A glossary example

As you can see, the glossary includes domain terms, such as *session* and *Q&A*, but also technical terms and acronyms, such as *UI* and *API*. We must never assume that all our stakeholders have got the same level of technical knowledge as us. We should also define any other process or methodology terms that may be unfamiliar to stakeholders. A very common occurrence is referring to the agile term **sprint** (from the Scrum framework). You'd be surprised by how many stakeholders think of a sprint as something that involves the development team running very quickly!

> **Important Note**
>
> Some processes and methodologies refer to the glossary as *ubiquitous language* or *common vocabulary*. Although the names may be different, the concept is the same.

Just like the stakeholder model, the glossary is a constantly evolving artifact. It keeps growing as our understanding increases. Having a rich glossary that is distributed to all stakeholders can save us many hours of unnecessary frustration and confusion. When we use domain terms in communication with our stakeholders, we must ensure that we are using them as defined in the glossary. The glossary also needs to be made available to all our stakeholders. Attaching it to a Specifications document and/or having it on the company Wiki will help towards that.

Once we have a first pass of our stakeholders model and a glossary that clarifies any critical domain terms, we can get on with eliciting and analyzing requirements.

Analyzing requirements

In *Chapter 1, The Requirements Domain*, we talked about the concept of the requirements funnel. This is a mental model that illustrates how requirements keep coming at us from many directions and in many forms and shapes. We need to filter these requirements and convert them to quantifiable and knowable entities so that we can process them. These items are our requirement domain entities (goals, stakeholders, capabilities, and features). If you've done chemistry at school, you may have used a separating funnel. These funnels are used to separate mixed liquids, such as oil and water. To convert requirements to requirement domain entities, we must use a mental separating funnel, which will filter the mixture of incoming requirements and then identify and create the relevant domain entities. Once we've done that, we can model those entities as an impact map, that is, our requirements model.

Our funnel will consist of distinct filtering techniques. These can be used separately, sequentially, or concurrently:

- A structured conversation
- D3
- Business process mapping

In the next few sections, we will explore these techniques in greater detail. We will begin by looking at having a **structured conversation**.

Having a structured conversation

Let's face it: having conversations is difficult. People tend to drift, topics are digressed from, and a myriad of other distractions may occur. A structured conversation is about focusing on specific aims and having a game plan when discussing requirements.

When should you use structured conversation? When having synchronous, interactive communication with the stakeholders, such as face-to-face, telephone, or internet meetings.

To have a fruitful conversation with the stakeholders and to be able to discern and capture their requirements, we need to structure our conversation with them in a very specific way:

1. Identify the type of stakeholder you are conversing with. If they are a business sponsor – in other words, a non-acting stakeholder – then their goals will be accomplished through the interaction of some actors with our system. For instance, a security officer will aim to preserve system security. Her goals will be achieved by affecting the interactions of other actors, such as the ones uploading files, doing audits, and so on. Make sure you identify those actors.

2. Identify the business or domain goals the stakeholder has, in the context of our system. The key questions here are *How do you think our system will benefit you in your role?* and *What would happen if our system was never delivered?* When you've identified the goals, make sure you validate them as explained in *Chapter 1, The Requirements Domain*, specifically the *Identifying goals* section. Good business goals have strategic value and result in a material outcome. If this isn't plain from our conversation, we need to press the issue until we define a valid and useful business goal. If the goal is a domain goal, make sure that it aligns with a valid business goal. Make sure you note any potential vanity or pet goals.

3. Ask the question, *What do you want to be able to do with our system that will help you achieve your goals?* Here, we're aiming to identify capabilities. Sometimes the stakeholder will start elaborating on their perceived way of achieving this capability, such as the functionality or system behavior or the features they want. At that point, we need to steer the conversation back toward *how* they want to achieve their goal through our system, not *what* our system will do. The *what* will be discussed later, when we are creating our system's features. Refer to *Chapter 2, Impact Mapping and Behavior-Driven Development*, for further guidance on identifying capabilities.

4. Once you have identified a capability, ask *Who else would benefit from this capability?* This is an opportunity to discover new stakeholders, who you might never have thought about otherwise. Let's say, for instance, that a lecturer needs the ability to search through loads of coursework, based on a topic or keyword, so that they can find and mark assessments quicker. The same capability may also be very useful to a student actor, who wants to review or correct their essays.

5. Once you have identified a capability, ask the stakeholder *What would you like the system to do in order to provide you this capability?* Then, go back to the development or product team and ask *What can we do / what are we technically able to do / what are we willing to do in order to provide this capability.* The intersection of the answer sets for these two questions is a good start for identifying our features.

The preceding steps are part of an interactive and incremental process. It is very rare that we'll nail down all the required capabilities in the context of the right stakeholders and business goals in one go. More often than not, our first conversation with the stakeholders will give us a rough idea of what's involved, while following conversations will help refine and increase our knowledge. The thing is, framing the conversation in terms of *What do you want to do with the system and why do you want to do it?* helps the stakeholders question their own assumptions and crystalize their expectations. It's a closed-loop feedback process. We break the loop only when both we and the stakeholder are satisfied that we accurately captured the *whos*, *hows*, and *whys*.

Once we have a reasonably well-defined view of business goals, stakeholders, capabilities, and some feature outlines, we can be satisfied that we have a good requirements model. We can then turn our attention toward creating our specifications, that is, toward refining our features, as we have already described in *Chapter 3, Writing Fantastic Features with the Gherkin Language.*

Decompose, Derive, Discover (D3)

Another technique for analyzing and discovering requirements is what I call D3 for short. D3 is about parsing the communications we receive so that we can capture the appropriate requirements domain entities and create our impact map.

When should you use D3? When we have asynchronous communication with the stakeholders (for example, email) or when we have written requirements (formal documents, business rules, examples, narratives, and so on). We can also apply D3 to visual requirements, such as screenshots or storyboards. We just have to create a written narrative based on those visualizations.

Decomposition

Decomposition is simply the process of breaking down a piece of text into its constituent parts. Decomposing a textual requirement helps us identify the requirements domain entities it is referring to. Before we learn how to decompose requirement text into its constituent domain entities, let's take a quick trip down memory lane and reminisce about our grammar classes at primary school.

In the English language, sentences are composed of clauses. A clause, at its minimum, is a group of words with a subject and a verb. A sentence will have at least one clause – for example, *Mark is looking at me*. However, most of the time the clause will have a subject, verb, object, and some object qualifiers – for example, *Jenny runs the meeting*, or *The cat sleeps on the purple mat*.

With this quick grammar lesson out of the way, let's find out how to detect entities in our written requirements.

Detecting actors

In a requirement description, the clause subject usually indicates an actor. For instance, in *The reviewer will be able to see the document's download speed*, the **reviewer** is our actor. Often, the subject is implied. For example, when we say, *The purchased items are listed on the orders page*, the implied subject is **the system**; it is the system that lists the items on the page. Our system is not an actor, as we have previously discussed in *Chapter 1, The Requirements Domain*, specifically the *Identifying stakeholders* section.

> **Tip**
>
> When the subject turns out to be the system, then in order to discover the actor, we need to find out who or what is affected or benefits by the action the system takes. So, if our requirement states "*the system will log all file download details*", our actor is likely to be the system administrator or whoever else benefits from that system activity.

Another important thing to consider when analyzing clauses is whether it involves an **active** or **passive** verb. When the verb is active, the subject of the verb is applying the action – for example, *Jack ate the pie*. When the verb is passive, the action is applied to the subject – for example, *The pie was eaten by Jack*. In *Jack ate the pie*, the subject is *Jack*. In *The pie was eaten by Jack*, the subject is *the pie*. So, here we have two clauses with the same meaning but different subjects. Here's the thing: actors are usually the subject of active verb clauses. To avoid confusion, it is good practice to convert passive clauses to active wherever possible. So, if you see a requirement that states *message is received*, translate this to *X receives message*. X is the subject, that is, our actor. You can then start asking questions about who or what exactly X is.

Detecting capabilities and features

The verbs and associated objects in a clause usually indicate an activity. So, in *The reviewer will be able to see the document's download speed*, the activity is *seeing download speed*. In *The purchased items are listed on the orders page*, the activity is *listing purchased items*.

Activities drive the discovery of features and capabilities. We can apply the criteria described in *Chapter 2, Impact Mapping and Behavior-Driven Development*, specifically the *Identifying capabilities and features* section, to determine that *Listing purchased items* and *Seeing download speed* are indeed features.

Sentences often consist of more than one clause, such as a main clause and some dependent clauses. A dependent clause is a clause that doesn't express a complete thought, so it can't stand alone but is used to qualify a main clause. For instance, when we say, *I will meet you at 9, unless the traffic is bad*, the *unless the traffic is bad* part is a dependent clause. Dependent clauses that begin with a subordinating conjunction (*because, although, when, unless, until, before, if*, and so on) tend to indicate feature scenarios. In *The customer can keep adding money to the bet until they reach their credit limit*, the main clause is *the customer can keep adding money to the bet* and the dependent clause is *until they reach their credit limit*. From the main clause, we can discern that we have a *Customer* actor and an *Add money to the bet* feature. The dependent clause tells us that we need to add a *Credit limit is reached* scenario to our feature.

Detecting goals

Occasionally, dependent clauses beginning with *because* or *so* will suggest an actor's goal. For instance, the requirement *The manager can see all transactions for the last year, so they can check if any transaction was unauthorized* reveals that the manager's goal is to check unauthorized transactions, that is, to prevent fraud. When you detect a goal, make sure to validate it with the stakeholders and also internally, as described in *Chapter 1, The Requirements Domain*.

Examples

Back in *Chapter 1, The Requirements Domain*, specifically the *The nature of requirements and specifications* section, we looked at some examples of different forms of requirements. Let's revisit some of these examples and analyze them with our new-found knowledge:

1. **Example 1**: Requirement as a formal statement – the system must provide a document searching facility.

    Analysis: The activity in this clause is *searching for documents*. This is a high-level, coarsely granular, and not directly actionable activity, which suggests that this is a capability.

The subject in this clause is *the system*. However, the system can never be an actor to itself. So, we need to find out who the real actors are. Let's say that, in this example, it will be the authors who want to be able to search the documents,

Detected entities:

- *Document search* (**capability**)
- *Author* (**actor**)

2. **Example 2**: Requirement as an example – Joe didn't have to pay for his coffee because it was his 11th one in that store.

    Analysis: The subject here is *Joe* and he is our actor. Obviously, *Joe* isn't a good name for an actor, so we will have to chat to our stakeholders to understand the role that Joe is playing in this example. We could then call our actor something like *Loyalty-card holder* or *Returning customer*.

    The activity Joe is undertaking is *paying for his coffee*. This is quite specific and directly actionable, so we put it down as a feature. The dependent conjunctive clause *because it was his 11th one in that store* suggests a scenario where Joe gets a free coffee after having bought 10 coffees.

    Detected entities:

- *Paying for coffee* (**feature**)
- *11th coffee in a row* (**feature scenario**)
- *Loyalty-card holder* (**actor**)

3. **Example 3**: Requirement as a business rule – accounts with monthly deposits larger than $1,000 are applied with a 2% higher interest by the system.

    Analysis: Since this is a passive-verb clause, let's re-write it in an active form:

    The system will apply 2% higher interest to accounts with balances greater than $1,000.

    The subject here is *the system*, so we can't use that as an actor. After talking with our stakeholders, we find out that the person affected by the system's activity (and therefore our actor) is the account holder.

    The activity here is *applying interest*. This is likely to be a feature, as it is quite specific, atomic, and directly actionable; that is, we can give this to our developers, alongside an interest rate and an initial amount, and they can implement this without too many questions. Since we now know that the actor involved in this feature is the account holder, we could call the feature *Account holder receives interest*.

The requirement also has a dependent conjunctive clause, as it's the same as saying that the interest will be applied *if the balance is greater than $1,000*. This suggests a scenario for our *applying interest* feature.

Detected entities:

- *Account holder* (**actor**)
- *Receive interest* (**feature**)
- *Balance greater than $1,000* (**feature scenario**)

Decomposition outcome

Decomposition allows us to identify requirements entities within raw text and create the basis for our model. For example, in our last example, the requirement was *The system will apply 2% higher interest to accounts with balances greater than $1,000.*

We decomposed it into its appropriate requirement entities, and we can now visualize it as an impact map:

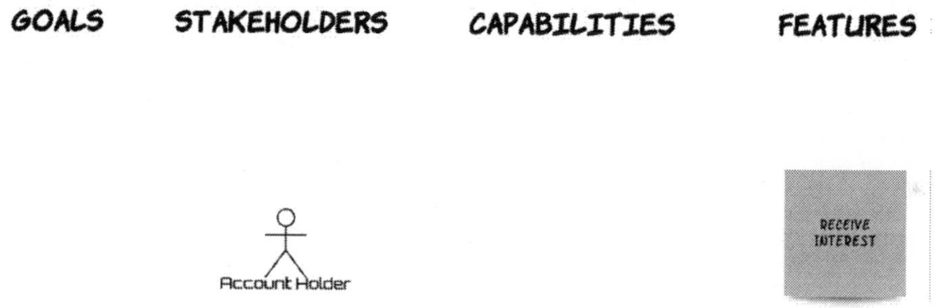

GOALS   STAKEHOLDERS   CAPABILITIES   FEATURES

Account Holder

RECEIVE INTEREST

Fig. 5.4 – Requirement decomposition

Our feature will look something like this:

```
Feature: Account holder receives interest
Scenario: Balance less than $1,000
   ...
Scenario: Balance greater than $1,000
   ...
```

At this stage, our model looks pretty bare. Remember, though, this is just the beginning of our analysis. Let's move onto the second phase.

Derivation

During decomposition, we identified a number of requirements entities, such as actors, capabilities, and features. If we put these entities on an impact map, chances are it will turn out to be an incomplete map, lacking the required hierarchical associations between our entities.

Our requirement entities do not exist in a bubble. Features are associated with capabilities. Capabilities serve some actor's goal. Derivation is simply the process of filling in the gaps in our impact map; in other words, this is where we derive our associated entities. To achieve that, we look at our impact map from right to left. Any features that we have identified must have a related capability. If they don't, then we need to either infer one or ideally go back to our stakeholders so that they can help us identify one.

Looking at the impact map for our example requirement from the previous section, we see that the right-most element is a feature. This *Receives interest* feature is a piece of functionality that is not associated with any greater impact the actor needs to have on our system, that is, a capability. This is where we go back to the actor or other stakeholders and try to understand which overarching system capability we're trying to deliver by implementing this feature. We cannot properly identify the capability until we understand the goal the actor is trying to accomplish.

Derivation outcome

A reasonable outcome of our derivation phase is that we derive the capability that our feature supports as the ability to *have financial incentives for opening an account with the bank*. This would help realize the bank's goal of trying to attract more customers by incentivizing the opening of new accounts. Our model now looks like this:

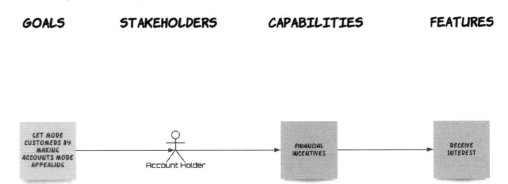

Fig. 5.5 – Requirement derivation

Although this is a much more complete model, we haven't finished yet. We'll be expanding our model during the discovery phase.

Discovery

In the decomposition phase, we got analytical. In the derivation phase, we got methodical. The discovery phase is where we get creative. This is where we discover new capabilities and features, based on the ones we have already detected and derived. In the derivation phase, we established the *Financial Incentives* capability, which will be delivered by implementing the *Receive Interest* feature. In the discovery phase, we ask the question, *Are there any other ways we can help deliver this capability?* That is, are there any other features that will help offer financial incentives to our account holder? After some thought (and consultation with our stakeholders), we decide that we could be offering cash-back to the account holders on selected purchases on their accounts. That's one more feature for our model.

Let's also consider our goal. Are there any other ways we can appeal to account holders, other than financial incentives? Why, yes there are. Turns out that our account holders would be motivated to open accounts with our bank if we also offered other services as part of our account package. We can identify two more features (travel insurance and fraud prevention) that can help deliver this capability.

Discovery outcome

After discovering our new entities, this is what our impact map model looks like:

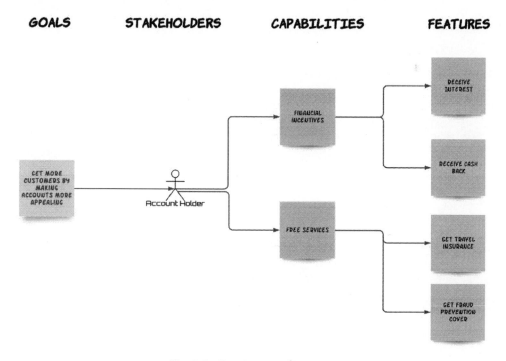

Fig. 5.6 – Requirement discovery

We started with a simple textual requirement and we ended up with a multi-level impact map with two capabilities and four features. We put our requirement through the requirements funnel, we applied the D3 filter, and we ended up with a structured, traceable, and clear representation of the requirement, which will form the basis of our specification and – ultimately – our delivered system.

We could actually go further with the discovery phase. We could easily discover other capabilities the account holder might need, even other actors who may benefit from these capabilities. It's like dominos (the game, not the pizza chain). Once the first few cards fall, then the whole stack goes. The discovery phase is an exciting and beautiful thing!

> **Tip**
> Wireframes and screen mock-ups can also be analyzed using D3. We first have to create a narrative based on the screens. Every button or checkbox we see will be pressed on certain conditions. Every text box will be filled with some meaningful text. Every link will lead us to another set of functionalities. Once we write all that down, we see that wireframes and mock-ups are just another set of statements, business rules, and examples. We can then start decomposing, deriving, and discovering domain entities based on that narrative.

One more technique for analyzing requirements is business process mapping. Let's look at it next.

Business process mapping

A business process is a sequence of related, structured activities or tasks by people or equipment that, when applied successfully, serves a particular business goal. Business processes, visualized as graphs, can be an extremely helpful tool in our analysis toolbelt. Business process diagrams are usually written using UML or BPMN notation, but simple flowcharts are also common.

> **Tip**
> When starting to elicit requirements, ask your client stakeholders whether they have already captured the business processes that they want our system to realize. If not, ask them whether any of their domain experts can possibly produce such diagrams. As well as helping you elicit requirements, this will also make them consider and evaluate their requirements much more carefully.

Let's take a look at a diagram for an order approval business process flowchart (courtesy of `https://commons.wikimedia.org/wiki/File:Approvals.svg`):

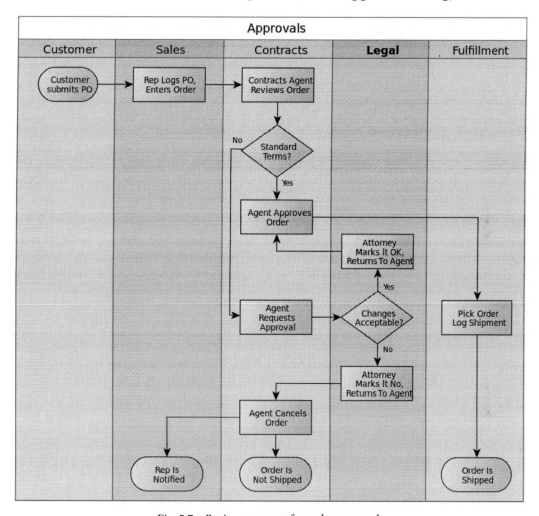

Fig. 5.7 – Business process for order approvals

Here we have five vertical lanes and a set of interconnected tasks, states, and decision points. This simple diagram can give us a lot of valuable information on our requirements analysis journey. There are some rules of thumb we can apply to map this business process to our standard requirement domain entities.

Here are those **business process mapping guidelines**:

- Business processes tend to represent high-level, transactional activities that help accomplish a business goal. If this sounds familiar, it's because we use similar terms to describe **capabilities**. That's right: often – but not always – business processes indicate capabilities. In our example, it would be reasonable to infer that we are dealing with an *order approval* capability. However, it's possible that we are dealing with a broader *order management* capability. The business process diagram gives the springboard needed so that we can have these conversations with the stakeholders.

- Lanes commonly represent an organizational role, that is, a **stakeholder**. Be wary, though, as lanes are sometimes used for other purposes too, such as to represent project phases. In our example, we can easily identify the following stakeholders: customer, sales rep, contracts agent, and attorney. We need to determine which of these will be interacting with our system in order to perform their responsibilities. These will be our actors.

- Tasks are usually equivalent to **features** or **scenarios**. Sometimes, tasks are so granular and simple that they are equivalent to a single step in a feature scenario. The *Agent approves order* task in our example business process appears to be nothing more than a scenario step. *Contract Agent review order*, however, looks more like a complete feature. Again, further conversations with the stakeholders will help us define the nature of these tasks.

- Decision points indicate the presence of divergent behavior, which points to different scenarios. For instance, the *Standard terms?* decision point in the business process diagram dictates two different scenarios for our *Contract Agent reviews order* feature: one where the order is written with standard terms and one where it isn't.

- **Goals** can be determined by considering the business process's goal, which is usually the final state of the process. In our example, this would be *Order is shipped*. So, the reason we go through the approval process is so that we can ship the order. It is obvious from examining the diagram that the order cannot be shipped without approval.

There are a couple of things to remember when applying these guidelines:

- These are heuristics, not absolute rules. They will apply to many situations and will help guide you in the right direction for many others. However, there will be some business processes where one or more of these guidelines will not apply. As always, use your common sense and ability to infer to spot these.

- Like every other technique or process described in this book, mapping business processes is an iterative and incremental procedure. Often, an understanding of a particular part of the business process will reveal itself only after we have clarified a different part of the process.

> **Tip**
> An important aspect of business process mapping is defining the scope of our system within the business process. A good way to accomplish this is to ask our client stakeholders to visually mark the diagram's lanes, tasks, and any decision points expected to be performed by our system. It's a quick and visible way of clarifying the scope and responsibilities of our system.

So, we are coming to the end of this chapter. Let's summarize what we have learned!

Summary

In this chapter, we discussed the importance of requirements elicitation and its current state in the agile world. We then learned how to create two important artifacts: the stakeholder model and the glossary. These artifacts give us the context and clarity of communication needed when communicating with stakeholders. Finally, we examined how to gather requirements from our stakeholders and analyze them in order to identify requirement entities. We learned a number of elicitation and analysis techniques, such as structured conversation, D3, and business process mapping. These techniques greatly facilitate the gathering and analysis requirements and allow their successful modeling in a requirements model.

This chapter also concludes the first part of the book. You now have enough knowledge to elicit, validate, model, and specify your system's requirements. However, requirements management doesn't stop here. In the next section of this book, we'll learn how to organize our requirement domain entities and work with them within agile processes and frameworks in order to deliver a system that works exactly as our stakeholders expect. Keep reading!

6
Organizing Requirements

In the previous chapters, we learned how to elicit and discover requirements, analyze them to identify requirement domain entities, model those entities and their relationships with an impact map, and capture system behavior in `Feature Scenarios`. At this point, we know how to create the following artifacts:

- Our requirements model as one or more impact maps
- Our specification as feature files
- A stakeholder or actor model
- A glossary

In this chapter, we will learn how to organize our existing artifacts and create some new ones. The aim is to increase the transparency and traceability of our methodology's outputs. This will give us the solid basis we need in order to start writing code that delivers the correct system. Specifically, we will look at the following:

- Providing easy access to our requirements model
- Ensuring traceability with entity identifiers
- Creating a specification document
- Creating a product backlog

By making our requirements model easily accessible and by creating a specification document that will be distributed to stakeholders, we are promoting transparency. Transparency builds confidence and is also a core Agile value. By adopting an entity identifier scheme for our requirements model, we are facilitating easy traceability between its entities. By creating a homogeneous and clutter-free backlog, we are promoting a visible list of what needs to be done that can be easily classified and prioritized. Let's start by looking at how to provide easy access to our requirements model.

Providing easy access to our requirements model

As mentioned in *Chapter 2, Impact Mapping and Behavior-Driven Development*, specifically the *Modeling Requirements with Impact Maps* section, our model is effectively a four-level tree structure. There are many tools that allow us to visually create tree structures, though I find mind-mapping tools ideally suited to the task. Some of the most popular ones are these:

- Lucidchart (`https://www.lucidchart.com/`): Online diagramming tool

- Draw.io (`https://draw.io`): Free, online diagramming tool

- MindMup (`https://www.mindmup.com/`): Online mind-mapping tool

- XMind (`https://www.xmind.net/`): Multi-platform mind-mapping tool

- GitMind (`https://gitmind.com/`): Free, online mind-mapping tool

Feel free to choose the tool you prefer, as long as it has good exporting and publishing functionality. We want to share our model with others, so we need to be able to export or publish it as an image, PDF, and ideally HTML, so that we can host it on a website. Many of these tools also provide cloud-hosting functionality whereby we can send our model on a cloud service such as Google Drive or OneDrive or even host it on a virtual cloud server. Once our model is in the cloud, it is very easy to share with our stakeholders and invite their comments and feedback.

Once we have made sure that our requirements model is visible and accessible to our stakeholders, there is one more thing we need to do to it: adopt an entity identifier scheme.

Ensuring traceability with entity identifiers

Our requirements model tree structure gives us a great way to visually track the relationships between our requirement entities. We can, at a glance, see all the capabilities needed to accomplish a stakeholder goal. We can also focus on a capability in order to immediately see all the `Features` we need to implement in order to provide it. There are, however, occasions when we need to reference a `Feature` outside the requirements model context. This could be, for example, in a conversation, an email, or some other document. Accurately referencing a `Feature` outside the requirements model can be tedious, as we need to use the full `Feature` name and provide some context to our reader or conversation partner. Similarly, we may mention a capability by its chosen name, but that makes it difficult for the other parties to relate it to a particular set of `Features`. An easy way to get around this problem is to assign identifiers to our capabilities and `Features`. The following figure presents a requirements model with assigned identifiers:

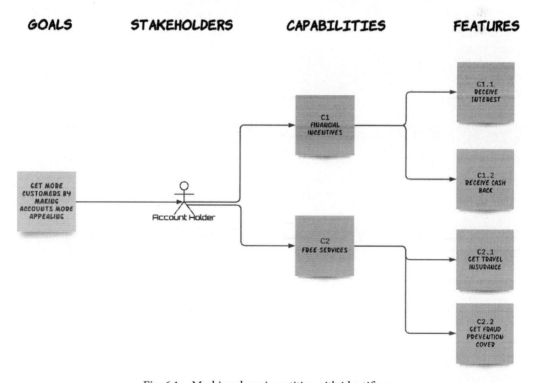

Fig. 6.1 – Marking domain entities with identifiers

Now, we can refer to the *Share Blog Posts* capability simply as C1. Not only is it shorter but it also allows our audience to easily identify all `Features` related to this capability, since their identifiers will be prefixed with **C1**. On the flip side, anyone coming across a **feature identifier** beginning with C1 will know exactly which capability this `Feature` helps deliver. When it comes to prioritizing and classifying our `Features` (as we will learn in *Chapter 7, Feature-First development*, and *Chapter 8, Creating Automated Verification Code*), having concise, meaningful identifiers can make a huge difference in productivity and avoid unnecessary confusion.

> **Important note:**
>
> You don't have to enumerate every capability identifier as C1, C2, and so on. Use whatever identification scheme is best understood by you and the stakeholders. For instance, instead of C1, we could have identified the *Share Blog Posts* capability as **ShareBlog**. Related `Features` could then be identified as *ShareBlog-1*, *ShareBlog-2*, and so on. Use any scheme that makes sense, as long as it's consistent and provides traceability between capabilities and `Features`.

It's now time to set our requirements model to one side and add some more transparency to our artifacts by creating the specification document.

Creating a specification document

We have written our system specification by fleshing out its behaviors as `Scenarios` in our `Features`. These can be seen by anyone who reads our feature files (`.feature`). The trouble is that our feature files are located in our project directory, alongside our code (see *Chapter 3, Writing Fantastic Features with the Gherkin Language*, specifically the *Knowing why Features are executable specifications* section). As our code will usually live on a hosted version control repository, such as GitHub or GitLab, making it accessible to all stakeholders can be challenging. To make our specification visible to anyone who wants to read it, it is a good idea to create a specification document. This document should include the following:

- **Revision history**: The specification document is a living document. It constantly changes and evolves. If our documentation system doesn't support versioning, then a revision history table is a good way of seeing how our Specification evolves over time.

- **Introduction**: An introduction explaining the purpose of the document, the intended readership, and any other pertinent information.

- **A list of related documents**: This should include links or references to any other documentation that may help readers better understand this document. This will usually be the raw requirement sources that were used to produce our specification, such as screenshots, wireframes, documents, diagrams, and so on.

- **The specification scope**: This would explain which release phase or product version this specification applies to.

- **Our glossary**: Our ubiquitous language, as discussed in *Chapter 5, Discovering and Analyzing Requirements*.

- **Our stakeholder or Actor model**: As well as the diagram, it is good practice to list the stakeholders and describe their roles or type of involvement with our system. This will help clarify any ambiguity and will help the readers better understand the Features.

- **A scope and capabilities section**: This should clarify the scope of the system (for example, MVP, version 1, and so on) and list the capabilities we are planning to deliver within this scope. These capabilities should be the ones we have captured in our requirements model, albeit only the ones within our current scope.

- **Assumptions, warnings, and constraints**: Although most of these should be documented within our Features, it is always good to outline the main ones in a separate section. We can also use this section for anything we haven't explicitly captured in the Features. For instance, this is where we can state that our system handles data in a GDPR-compliant manner (https://gdpr.eu/what-is-gdpr), or that our system will be hosted in specific geographic regions.

- **Features**: These should be a copy of our feature files' content. Nothing more and nothing less.

- **Appendices**: Sometimes, we may wish to explain a particular business process we captured or expand on a user workflow improvement our system enacts. Basically, anything that may be useful to the reader but is not appropriate for any other section of our Specification goes into an appendix.

> **Important note:**
>
> Features in our specification document and Features in our project code directory must always be synced. This can be achieved either manually or by writing automated scripts that perform the syncing (depending on the abilities of your documentation software or host).

The purpose of the specification document is to have a single, visible, easily accessible source of truth for what our system will do and how it will behave. It should give any of its readers, regardless of their level of technical expertise, a comprehensive idea of what our system does, why it does it, and who is involved in our system and how.

Our specification document doesn't actually need to be a physical document. It could be a hosted website or part of the company's wiki. The important thing is that it's always visible to, and easily accessible by, all our stakeholders. Part of the reason why it should be so is that our stakeholders will need to review and agree to it.

Getting stakeholder agreement on the specification

One of the reasons why we need to make the specification document visible easily accessible is that it needs to be constantly reviewed by the relevant stakeholders. These will usually be our client-side stakeholders, who provided us with the requirements. In this document, we are telling our clients, "*We received your requirements, and this is what we are going to do to address them.*" By reading agreeing to it, our clients are telling us, "*We think this specification will realize our requirements, within its scope, and we accept it.*" Agreement doesn't necessarily have to be given on the whole document. Often, the stakeholders will approve only some of the Features in the specification. Once a feature has been approved, we have the green light to go ahead with its development. The specification forms the basis of our interactions with the stakeholders. It gives both them and the development team the clarity, confidence, and alignment of aims needed to deliver a successful project.

Scoping the specification

In today's agile world, we tend to work in an iterative and incremental manner. That means we tend to release software often. It also means we tend to do phased or versioned releases. That is, we deliver some Capabilities – or part of some – in version 1, and then some more in version 2, and so on and so forth. At the same time, we may also be doing minor releases to our clients, mainly for demonstration and feedback purposes. We should scope our specification document for the major releases, the v1.x versions, and not every little code drop we put out there for *show and tell*. As a result, we should expect to have multiple specification documents for each major phase, version, or release. Each of these documents will detail the capabilities and Features needed for that particular scope.

At the same time that we are working on the specification document, we should also be thinking about creating a list of all the Features we need in order to deliver a working system. We call this list the product backlog.

Creating a product backlog

A **product backlog** is simply a list of all the Features that we, the system builders, need to implement in order to successfully deliver the system. In order to understand the role and significance of the backlog, we need to understand how the **Software Development Life Cycle (SDLC)** works.

The Agile SDLC

The SDLC consists of three major phases, as depicted in the following diagram:

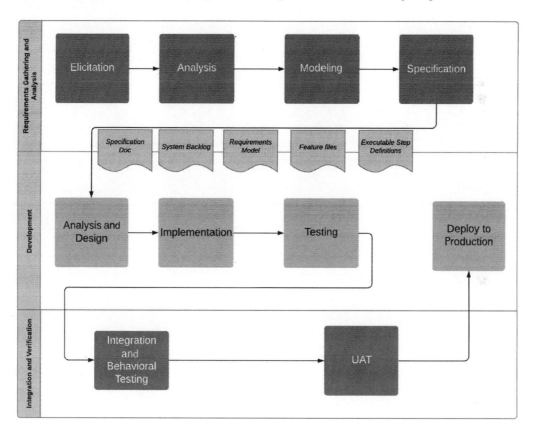

Fig. 6.2 – SDLC

These phases are as follows:

- Requirements gathering and analysis
- Development
- Integration and verification

In Agile development, these three phases are not singular. They are repeated in continuous iterations, each iteration focusing on specific functionality or goals. Neither are they sequential; they can and do occur in parallel. Within the same iteration, a team member may be doing requirements gathering, while a second one writes code for a feature and a third team member verifies a different feature. In short, Agile development happens in an *iterative and incremental* way. Each iteration implements some features and builds upon what the previous iteration produced.

So far, in this book, we have operated at the requirements gathering and analysis phase. We have learned how to produce the following artifacts:

- **A requirements model**: An impact map that provides visibility and traceability of our requirements.

- **Feature files**: A detailed and structured description of our system's behaviors, that is, our specification. Feature files are mainly for the development team's benefit. They are embedded in our system's code base and connect our implementation with our specification.

- **Executable step definition files**: These are code files that are directly associated with feature files. A step definition file contains code that exercises our system's behavior and verifies it.

- **A specification document**: Mostly for our stakeholders' benefit, it includes the feature file content, as well as the stakeholder model, the glossary, and other relevant and useful information.

To truly support an iterative and incremental development cycle, we need to be able to prioritize and classify what goes into our iterations and increments. To do that, we need a product backlog. Let's consider how to decide what to put into our backlog.

What goes into the product backlog?

Suppose we are starting work on the first iteration of our project. Using our knowledge from the previous chapters of this book, we have done the following:

- Gathered requirements from our stakeholders

- Used analytical techniques, such as D3, to map the requirements into goals, stakeholder capabilities, and features, that is, a requirements model

- Used our requirements model to validate existing requirements and derive new ones

- Used fundamental principles and applied patterns to correctly sketch out system behaviors (our `Feature Scenarios`)
- (Optionally) Written step definition code that verifies our `Feature`

We are now ready to start the development phase of our iteration. This is where the development team looks at `Features` and decides how to implement them. The first stage of the development phase is the analysis and design stage. This stage results in the creation of a number of **tasks**. Tasks are usually development-related, but they could also be about infrastructure, logistics, and other things. In short, a task is something needed to be done in order to implement a Feature. Let's take a look at one of our previously demonstrated `Features`, the *Create a Blog Post* feature. A quick analysis will result in a number of tasks, such as the following:

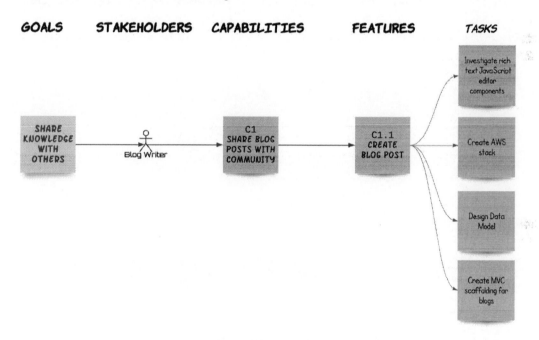

Fig. 6.3 – Feature analysis results in task creation

The important thing to keep in mind about tasks is that they are transient. They are only important while they are incomplete. Once they are done, we don't really care about them much. They have reached the end of their usefulness.

Once we start working on our tasks, implementing our `Features`' behavior, it is inevitable that we will start getting **bugs**. Bugs are faults or defects with our system's implementation or design, which cause our system to behave unexpectedly or erroneously. Getting bugs is a normal part of the development process and nothing to be feared or frowned upon. We will examine different ways of dealing with bugs when we look at leveraging different Agile frameworks in *Chapter 7, Feature-First Development*. For now, though, the important thing is to remember that bugs, like tasks, are transient. Here today, gone tomorrow. What remains is our features. Features drive our development, they describe our system's behavior, they are the distillation of the requirements elicitation and analysis phase, and they remain when tasks and bugs are gone.

When it comes to the crunch, it doesn't matter how many tasks we have completed or how many bugs we have fixed. What matters is how many features we have implemented and, by extension, which capabilities we delivered. This is what our stakeholders expect, and this is what we get paid for. It is therefore fitting that our backlog focuses on and contains only `Features`. It is wise to prioritize the `Features` in our backlog, as illustrated in the following example:

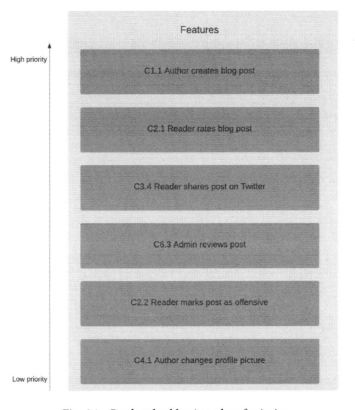

Fig. 6.4 – Product backlog in order of priority

Our backlog is a list of items (also known as **cards**) representing a **Feature**. In this diagram, we have placed the highest-priority features near the top of our backlog. We could also classify our backlog features; an easy way to do this is by using different background colors for different categories. We could classify features by difficulty level, related capabilities, benefit to stakeholders, completion level, and many other ways. The important thing is that our backlog should give us all the information we need at a glance.

Tip:

The product backlog is a live artifact. It changes and evolves along with our understanding of the system. Features will constantly be getting added to, or removed from, it. The backlog should be owned and maintained by a person with a good understanding of both the stakeholder's requirements and vision and your organization's mission and resources, such as the product owner (if using Scrum) or someone in a similar role.

It is also imperative that the cards on our backlog lead directly to our feature details. We can achieve that by embedding the feature file within the `Feature` card itself or just providing a link to it.

Where to keep the backlog

Our backlog will contain all the features we need to implement for our system, and it will help us prioritize and classify them. However, we will also need to track the progress of the features we are working on. For that reason, our backlog list will usually be part of a larger list of lists, such as a Kanban board or a Scrum board, as in the following figure:

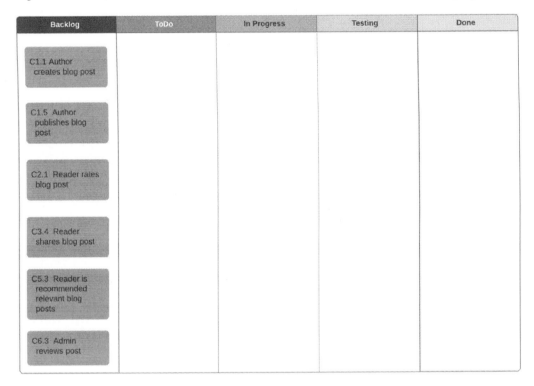

Fig. 6.5 – Product backlog on a task board

This makes it easy to simply drag selected features into the **ToDo** column, which is the starting point for many Agile methodologies. There are many tools that support the creation and maintenance of task boards, such as Pivotal Tracker, Asana, Jira, Monday. com, Trello, and many, many others. Choose whichever one takes your fancy as long as it matches all your other development needs and fits in with your Agile framework of choice (Scrum, Kanban, Crystal, and so on).

Summary

In this chapter, we learned how to create a specification document and a product backlog. We also learned about some practical and logistical tweaks in order to ensure that our produced artifacts are transparent and provide traceability. The transparency of our outputs is a crucial aspect of delivering a successful system. If our stakeholders find it difficult to understand what we are doing and how our system will behave, then we risk losing their confidence in us and our system as well as the communication channels that provide us with requirements and feedback. The specification document goes a long way toward providing everything the stakeholders need to know about our system in a single, visible, and accessible location.

Traceability is also an essential part of our methodology. One of the many benefits of impact mapping is that we can trace a feature all the way to an underlying stakeholder's goal, and vice versa. Our development team knows exactly what the impact is of a task or a Bug they're working on, on the business and the client. Everyone involved in the project can see the big picture, as well as the small details. Entity identifiers help take this traceability one step further and ensure that we always have a context for our features.

Finally, we saw how having a feature-based product backlog provides a clean way, compatible with an agile SDLC, to track all the important things we need to do in order to realize our stakeholders' goals. In the next chapter, we will see how to leverage our backlog when applying our requirements methodology within some of the most popular Agile methods.

7

Feature-First Development

So far in this book, we've learned all about analyzing and modeling requirements, turning them into executable specifications, that is, features, and organizing our specifications into a system backlog. This chapter is about the next step: turning our specifications into working, delivered software. We will see how to integrate our features within the two most popular Agile approaches to software development, the Scrum framework, and the Kanban method. We will learn how to create and manage a task board and how to use it as a springboard to deliver the software we have specified in our features, while effectively dealing with change. Specifically, we will learn about the following topics:

- Setting up for successful delivery

- Effecting just-in-time development

- Working with Scrum

- Working within Kanban

By the end of the chapter, you will know how to leverage accurate, durable, and well-scoped features – that you will know how to create – as the basis for the controlled and phased delivery of working software. Let's begin with the pre-requisites.

Setting up for successful delivery

Before we can embark on our development effort, we need to have in place the necessary infrastructure that will help us successfully deliver our system's capabilities.

Creating a staging environment

Software teams tend to use different environments under which they work at different stages of the development life cycle. An environment consists of the hardware, software, and configuration needed to develop and deploy our system. The development team usually works under a development environment, which includes the various tools and configurations needed for software development. When the system is about to be deployed, these tools are no longer required, so the system is deployed to other environments that are much more restricted, so as to emulate the target deployment environment more realistically.

In the context of the methodology presented in this book, we will need a dedicated environment on which to verify our delivered system against the specifications, that is, a staging environment.

A staging environment is an almost exact replica of the production environment where our system will be deployed and used. It requires a copy of the same configurations of hardware, servers, databases, and caches as the production environment. The only difference between the staging and production environments is the data they contain. Real customer data must not be exposed on the staging environment, for privacy and compliance reasons, if nothing else. Instead, we copy customer data with all sensitive or personal data changed or otherwise obfuscated. We can then use this data to verify our system's behavior, without exposing sensitive information. Once we have somewhere to host and test our code, we need to be able to manage its development.

Creating a task board

A task board is where we track the progress of our features' development. Task boards are sometimes referred to as **Scrum boards** or **Kanban boards** (depending on whether they're being used under the Scrum or Kanban approaches), but the concept is the same—a list of columns representing the different stages of the development life cycle for our deliverable items. Items on a task board are usually represented as cards. Each card has a title, description, and other metadata, and can be colored and labeled in different ways.

Task boards are not strictly defined. Some have fewer columns than others. Some have differently named columns. It all comes down to what is important to the team and organization using them. What they all have in common, however, is that they allow us to visualize our workflow, to know how our team is doing and to get a feel for the direction our development is heading.

In this book, we shall be using the following six-column task board:

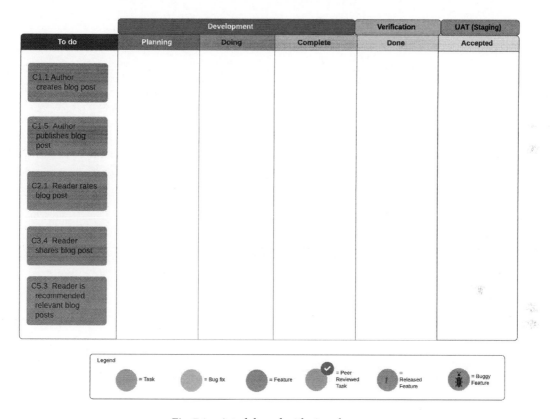

Fig. 7.1 – A task board with six columns

Let's examine its columns more closely:

- **To do**: This is the feeder column for our development cycle. This where we put the features that we select for current development from our backlog. The number of features we can put in here depends on the agile framework or methodology we are applying, as we shall see in the following sections. Only fully-formed features, that is, the features with a complete set of scenarios for our scope, can reside in this column.

- **Planning**: This is where we put the features we have started working on. When we put a feature in this column, we start analyzing it and producing a number of tasks necessary to implement the feature. Those tasks will be added to the **Planning** column too.

- **Doing**: Any tasks or bugs we started working on are moved into this column. They stay here until they are complete.

- **Complete**: When a developer working on a task or bug deems it to be complete then they move it to this column. Any card in this column will be subject to code reviews by the rest of the development team. This will also usually include checking that any unit tests for this card are passing.

- **Done**: When a task or bug has been reviewed and checked, then it's time to move it to the **Done** column. When all tasks or bugs related to a feature have been moved to this column, then that means that the feature is ready for verification. We can now run our automated step definitions using *Cucumber*, *JBehave*, *Jasmine*, among others. They will hopefully tell us that our feature is behaving as expected, that is, it is done.

- **Accepted**: After our feature is done, we deploy it to the staging environment, and we invite the relevant actors and other stakeholders to use it. Once they are all happy with the feature, we move it to the **Accepted** column.

Now that we know how to use our task board, let's look at one more thing we need to do before we start our system development.

Defining done

The ultimate aim of a development cycle is to implement the features in our backlog. This raises the question, *How can we tell if a feature is done?* Is it when the development team tells us that it's *done*? Is it when the testing team tells us so? Can we apply some criteria to it?

These are questions that have plagued many a development team throughout the years. This has led some Agile frameworks and methodologies to emphasize the importance of defining *done*. This is what the Scrum Guide (`https://www.scrum.org/resources/scrum-guide`) has to say on the matter:

> *When a product backlog item or an Increment is described as done, one must understand what done means. Although this may vary significantly for every Scrum Team, members must have a shared understanding of what it means for work to be completed and to ensure transparency. This is the definition of done for the Scrum Team and it is used to assess when work is complete on the product increment.*

Since, following the methodology in this book, we are leveraging BDD and writing our features as executable specifications, we already have a clear and concise definition of done:

A feature is done when all of its scenarios have been verified.

In *Chapter 3, Writing Fantastic Features with the Gherkin Language* in the *Features are Executable Specifications* section, we talked about creating step definitions. This is the code that verifies each step in our scenarios against a delivered system. This is where step definitions come into their own. By using a BDD-aware tool, such as Cucumber, JBehave, Jasmine, and others, we can automatically verify whether our system behaves the way we said it would. It's an easy and objective way of knowing whether a feature is "done" or not. Auto-verification using Cucumber and similar tools can be done by anyone and produces legible, formatted output that can be read by anyone. Most of these tools can produce HTML reports, which can then be hosted on a website.

But even if you didn't get to write step definitions for your executable specifications, do not despair. All it takes is for someone to use the system while looking at the features (which are also contained in the specifications document). They can then manually verify whether a feature works or not.

Once we have all the pre-requisites in place, we can start our development process. But before we jump into that, let's take a quick look at the drive and motivation behind what we're about to do.

Actualizing just-in-time development

When people are first introduced to a feature-only backlog, they tend to ask questions like, *But what about research tasks or spikes (product testing tasks in order to explore alternative solutions)?*, *What about generic tasks like applying style sheets?*, or *We need a separate task for setting up a Continuous Integration pipeline.* The response to all these concerns is always the same:

Tasks do not exist in a bubble. We are only doing things that help to implement a feature. If a task doesn't contribute toward a feature, then we should not be working on it.

As discussed in *Chapter 3, Writing Fantastic Features with the Gherkin Language*, features can reflect both functional and non-functional aspects of a functionality. So, that research you want to do into different indexing engines is almost certainly tied to a search-related feature somewhere in your backlog. If you start working on this task, it means you start working on that feature and that feature should be in the **To do** column. Those stylesheets you want to apply across the website help to implement a specific feature. If you don't have any features for these tasks, then now's the time to create some. The same goes for that **Continuous Integration** and **Continuous Delivery (CI/CD)** pipeline you want to set up. Having a CI/CD pipeline is extremely useful in an agile development life cycle. It is also a task that will be important to most of the features in your backlog. As explained in the upcoming *Sprint development cycle* section, generic tasks like this one apply to many features and can be denoted as such. You just need to know the feature in the **To do** column that's going to be the first to benefit from this task. As stated, no task lives in a bubble.

This feature-first approach contributes to a generic paradigm that I call **Just-in-Time (JIT)** development. JIT development helps focus the software production line on the most important things first. It helps deliver the software that is needed when it is needed. Often in agile development, the traditional product backlog will carry a large number of diverse and widely scoped tasks or user stories. This makes the backlog difficult to manage, prioritize, and plan for. By eliminating tasks that do not need to be in the backlog, we effectively eliminate waste, we increase our planning and delivery efficacy, and we help focus our team and our stakeholders on the ultimate prize: *helping our stakeholders achieve their goals by delivering needed capabilities, implemented through features.*

A feature-first approach fits in perfectly with the agile and lean philosophies of reducing waste and embracing simplicity. In the next two sections, we'll see how we can apply it within the scope of the two most popular agile approaches, Scrum and Kanban.

Working with Scrum

Scrum is the most popular agile approach. Scrum is a process framework that is fully centered around iterative and incremental delivery. A delivery iteration in Scrum is called a **Sprint** and it lasts between 2-4 weeks.

The Scrum framework consists of three components:

- **The Scrum team**: A self-organizing, cross-functional set of people who will deliver the working software. The team consists of the *product owner*, the *Scrum master*, and the *development team*.

- **Scrum events**: A number of time-boxed events that help create regularity, promote and provide feedback, foster self-adjustment, and promote an iterative and incremental life cycle. These events include *Sprint Planning, Daily Scrum, Sprint Review*, and *Sprint Retrospective.*

- **Scrum artifacts**: Items that represent work or added value and that provide transparency for the team's work progress and achievements. The Scrum artifacts are the *product backlog*, the *Sprint backlog*, and the *increment*, which is the software that needs to be delivered for the Sprint.

Scrum does not prescribe any development methodologies or task management processes. How to design and develop our code and how to manage our tasks is left up to us. There are certain practices that most Scrum teams use, like test-driven development or story-point estimating, but these are not mandated by the Scrum framework. We will see how our requirements management methodology output fits within Scrum in the subsequent sections.

Sprint planning

The Sprint planning event signals the start of a new Sprint. The development team, in conjunction with the product owner, select which features to move from the backlog into the **To do** column of the task board. This doesn't happen randomly. There are a number of rules for how and which features are moved into the **To do** list:

- **Priority**: Features are selected according to their priority, which is decided by the product owner. They are also selected so that they satisfy a theme or goal for that Sprint. This could be something like *Enable blog sharing on social media* or *Recommend relevant content to blog reader*. This is where our requirements model really comes in handy. We have already derived our features from capabilities. A capability can easily serve as a Sprint theme. This makes it easy to select features, as we already know which features we need to deliver a capability for. In addition, capabilities are directly related to goals, so our product owner can use that to help set the Sprint goal. All the analytical work we did in creating our requirements model is now paying dividends for our development process too.

- **Load Capacity**: The number of features moved to the **To do** column is limited by the development's team constraint of how much work they can handle in a Sprint. This is usually measured by a metric called *velocity*. Velocity is a measure of the amount of work a team can tackle during a single Sprint. Velocity is determined and refined after the completion of many Sprints. As part of the Sprint planning event, the development team will have to estimate the effort involved in implementing a feature and decide whether they can take it on as part of the upcoming Sprint.

- **Fully-formedness**: Only features with full contextual information and detailed scenarios (as described in *Chapter 3, Writing Fantastic Features with the Gherkin Language*, in the *Writing a fully-formed feature* section), can be moved to the **To do** column.

- **UI guidelines**: Many, if not most, of our features will involve direct interaction with an actor through a UI. There are many ways in which the functionality implemented in a feature can be invoked by and presented to an actor. This is why it is very important that such features are accompanied by screen mock-ups or wireframes that allow us to aim for specific UI layout and styling.

> **Important note:**
> The **To do** column of the task board is usually referred to as the **Sprint backlog** when using Scrum.

Sprint development cycle

The aim of a Sprint is to move all features from the **To do** column to the **Accepted** column within the Sprint's duration. During the Sprint, the development team will examine the features in the **To do** column and will come up with a set of tasks required to implement these features. These tasks are placed in the **Planning** column. Tasks associated with a feature are referenced with that feature's identifier. Some tasks will be associated with more than one feature. Multiple feature identifiers should then be used.

> **Tip:**
> Some tasks will be universal, that is, they will be required by all our features. Usually, these tasks are things like setting up a database, a cloud-server instance, or some other generic or infrastructure task. It's good practice to use a generic identifier for these tasks (I personally prefer the asterisk (*) symbol) so that these tasks can be given due attention and priority.

When developers start actively working on a task, they move it to the **Doing** column. When the task is complete, that is, the developer is assured the task is finished, the task is moved to the **Complete** column. The task is then peer-reviewed. If the peer review outcome is that modification is needed to the task, then it is moved back to the **Planning** or **Doing** columns (dependent on the level of modification required).

Tasks that are reviewed successfully are labeled as *checked* and remain in the **Complete** column until all the tasks required by a particular feature are **Complete**. We then verify that feature by executing its specification, that is, its feature file, with a BDD tool such as Cucumber, JBehave, and so on. Alternatively, we can verify the feature manually, simply by running our feature code and checking that it does what it says in our specification.

If the feature is verified it is then moved to the **Done** column. Once in the **Done** column, it is the development team's responsibility to ensure the feature is deployed to the staging area where our stakeholders can use it and give us their feedback. Since our feature has been already verified against the specification, and the specification has been agreed with the stakeholders, the feedback we should be getting at that stage should be limited to minor usability issues. In most cases, the stakeholder should be happy with the feature, in which case we move it into the **Accepted** column.

If the feature is not verified, that is, our Cucumber run fails, then we need to determine the cause of failure. The feature will stay in the **To do** column and we may add new tasks to the **Planning** column in order to address the cause of the verification failure.

If the feature is verified but the stakeholder refuses to accept it, there are three probable causes:

- Some system behavior doesn't match the stakeholder's expectation. This should be a rare occurrence. It means our specification is wrong. We have probably violated some basic principles or applied some anti-patterns (very likely the *Vague Outcomes* one) when writing our feature. We need to go back to our specification and fix it. The feature will go back to the **To do** column.

- There is some usability issue. This is the most common cause of non-acceptance. Our specification is basically accurate, but we may need to enhance or expand it. If the issue is simply UI-related, for example, layout or styling, then we leave our feature in the **Done** column and we create a new task under **Planning** in order to fix the issue. If the issue is one of usability affecting behavior, for example, non-accessible color schemes, or a lack of keyboard shortcuts, then we put the feature back in the **To do** column and we change the specification to include the desired behavior.

- There is a bug in our system. Our specification is accurate but there may be a bad code line or a badly designed component that causes our system to behave inconsistently under certain circumstances. We leave our feature in the **Done** column and we create a new task under **Planning** in order to fix the bug.

The workflow algorithm described in this section can be illustrated by the following flowchart:

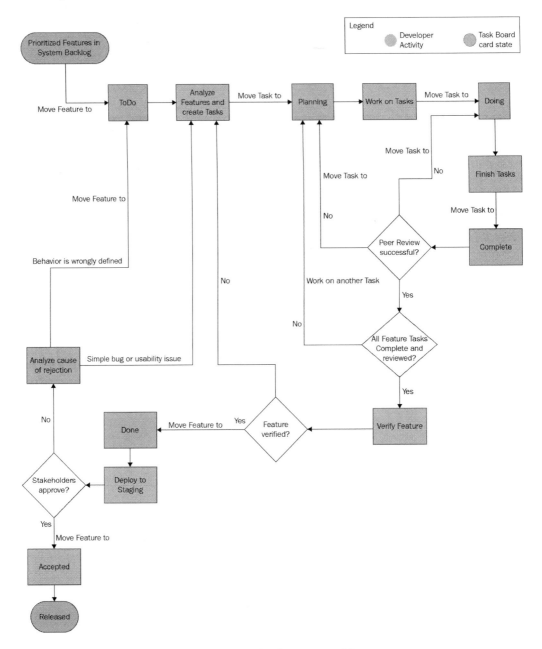

Fig. 7.2 – Sprint development workflow

The preceding diagram is just a visual representation of everything mentioned so far in this section.

Our task board during the Sprint development will look something like this:

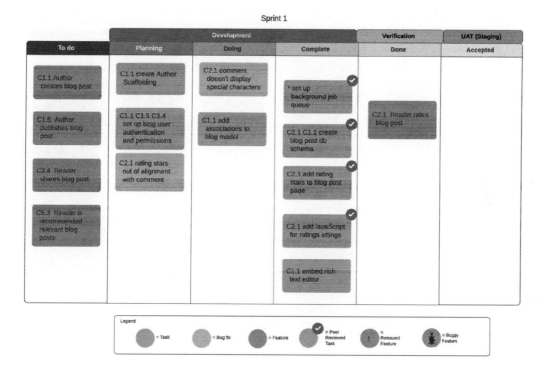

Fig. 7.3 – Task board during Sprint development

As you can see, features reside in the **To do** column and they are moved to the **Done** and **Accepted** columns as necessary. The development-type columns (**Planning**, **Doing**, **Complete**) are for development-related items only, such as tasks and bug fixes. This provides a clear and useful separation between the items incidental to development and items critical to the project and stakeholders, that is, the features.

End of Sprint

At the end of the Sprint period, our Sprint will be in one of two states.

Completed Sprint

In a completed Sprint, all features are in the **Accepted** column and all tasks/bugs are in the **Complete** column, as depicted in the following diagram:

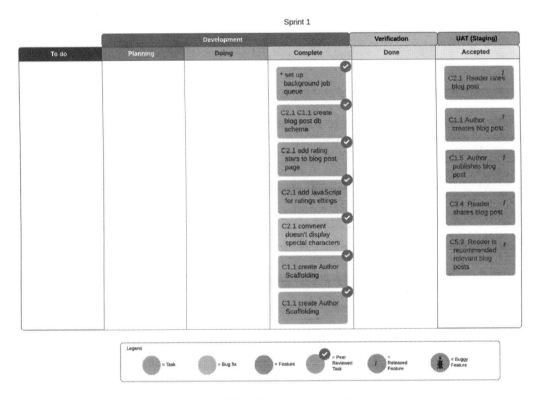

Fig. 7.4 – Task board for a completed Sprint

This means that our Sprint has been successful. We can now reset the board, as follows:

1. We remove items from the **Complete** column. Some people prefer to add an **Archived** column on their task board, into which they place all completed tasks and bugs. Many tools, like Trello, offer a built-in archiving functionality.

2. We mark the features in the **Accepted** column with the Sprint number and move them back to our system backlog. The Sprint number is effectively a release number for our feature and helps us track when a feature has been delivered, as well as its context (the Sprint goal).

At the end of a completed Sprint, our task board should be empty again, waiting for the next Sprint.

Incomplete Sprint

If at the end of the Sprint, there is at least one feature in the **To do** or **Done** columns, as illustrated in the following board, then the Sprint is incomplete:

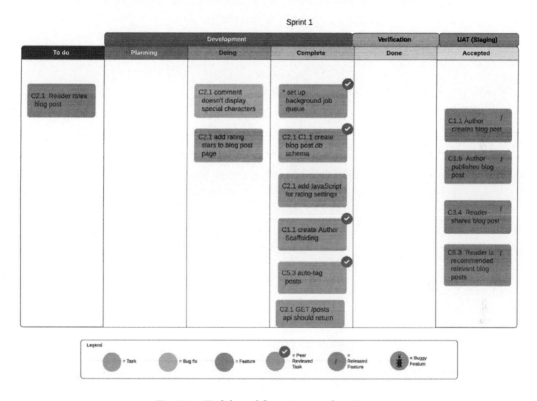

Fig. 7.5 – Task board for an incomplete Sprint

In this case, we do the following:

1. Archive all cards in the **Complete** column.

2. Mark the features in the **Accepted** column with the Sprint number and move them back to our system backlog.

3. Move cards from the **Doing** column back to the **To do** column.

In our preceding example board, that would mean that after tidying up, our board would have three cards in the **To do** column: the C2.1 feature, task, and bug. Any features not completed in a Sprint are almost always scheduled for the next Sprint. This is reflected in our board management process.

> **Tip:**
> In the unlikely event that the product owner decides an unfinished feature will not be in the next Sprint, move the feature back in the backlog and mark the related tasks/bugs as "Dropped" before archiving them. That way, you'll be able to easily retrieve them in the future, if needed.

Next, let's see what happens when things change unexpectedly during our development cycle.

Dealing with change

One of the constant risks in every line of work is dealing with change. We can't control the way things change but we can be prepared and be adaptable to anything new coming our way. Scrum tries to control change by discouraging changes that distract from the Sprint goal or theme. Once the development team commits to a Sprint, then it should try to reach the Sprint goal, or – if it realizes it can't – it should abort the Sprint.

What that means with respect to the methodology presented in this book is that once all features in the **To do** column, that is, the Sprint backlog, have been agreed upon, then no new features should be added during the Sprint. We can, though, add new tasks mid-Sprint if that's when we realize that we need them in order to implement a feature that's currently in the Sprint **To do** column.

Inevitably in our development life cycle, we will get a number of **Change Requests (CRs)** from our client-facing stakeholders. CRs usually tend to cover three types of changes:

- Emergent bugs, that is, bugs discovered after a code release.
- Behavioral changes, when already agreed, accepted, and delivered features need to be modified.
- New behaviors, that is, new requirements.

Dealing with new requirements is something we've been addressing a lot in this book. You should know the drill by now:

1. Analyze and map the requirements, as described in *Chapter 4, Crafting Features Using Principles and Patterns*, in the *Discovering requirements* section.

2. Model the requirements, as detailed in *Chapter 2, Impact Mapping and Behavior-Driven Development*.

3. Describe the new features, as explained in *Chapter 3, Writing Fantastic Features with the Gherkin Language*, and *Chapter 4, Crafting Features Using Principles and Patterns*.

4. Finally, just add the new features to the system backlog.

For the rest of this section, we'll deal with the other two types of change.

Emergent bugs

So far, we have seen how to deal with bugs occurring within a Sprint, as part of a feature implementation. But what happens if someone finds a bug with an already released feature? An emergent bug is not immediately obvious after feature delivery but usually surfaces after a certain number of functionality repetitions, certain data/user loads, or when exercising some extreme scenarios. In such a case, the first thing to do is to mark the feature as *buggy* in our backlog. Again, adding labels or color-marking is a great, visual way of marking a card. We should also add some comments on that feature's card, describing the bug or referencing a bug tracking database.

> **Important note:**
> If the bug is deemed by the stakeholders as critical or high priority, and is caused by some scenario that we haven't captured in our feature, we must add that scenario to our feature. Any behavior that is significant in the business domain should be represented in our specification.

It is now up to the product owner to decide in which Sprint to fix that bug. They will have to re-prioritize that feature in the backlog and decide when to put it into the **To do** column during Sprint Planning. The development team will then treat that feature like any other feature in the **To do** column. The only difference is that the generated tasks will be focused on fixing that bug, instead of re-creating feature functionality from scratch.

The following diagram illustrates such an example:

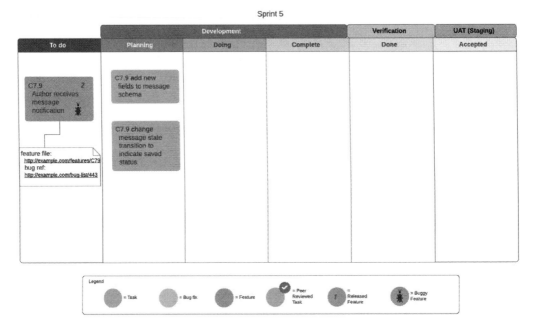

Fig. 7.6 – Dealing with emergent bugs – start of Sprint

The task board in this image is being used to plan Sprint number 5. The product owner has decided that in this Sprint, we should be fixing a bug reported in relation to feature C7.9. That feature was delivered during Sprint 2, as per the card label. A bug was reported in relation to this feature, so it has been already been marked as **defective (buggy)** in the backlog. A reference to the bug details has been included in the card's details. The development team has analyzed the bug and decided it can be fixed by doing two things, which they have captured as two tasks. They have already made changes to the feature's affected scenarios, which are detailed in a link included in the card's details. They can now start working on these tasks and move them through the **Doing** to **Complete** columns. They can then verify the feature by running its executable steps. By the end of the Sprint, the task board should look like this:

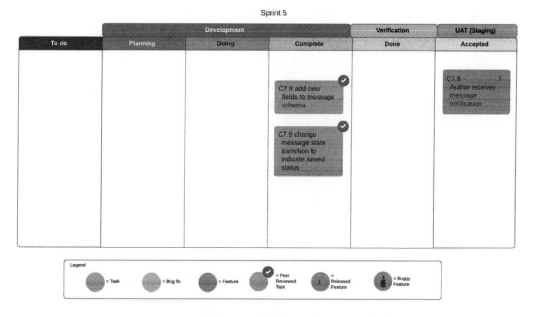

Fig. 7.7 – Dealing with emergent bugs – end of Sprint

The bug has been fixed. Our feature is now in the **Accepted** column. It is no longer marked as buggy and its release number has changed to the current Sprint, that is, number 5. We can now move the feature back to the bottom of our backlog and make ourselves a deserved cup of tea.

Changes to existing behavior

Sometimes, it may turn out that some behavior that we specified and agreed with our stakeholders is based on false assumptions and needs to be changed after our feature has been accepted and released. In such a case, our stakeholders will request that we make a change to the feature. Dealing with such changes is not much different than dealing with emergent bugs. They both necessitate some changes to our feature, but each is presented in different contexts. In terms of task management, however, we deal with behavioral changes in exactly the same way we deal with bugs. The practical differences are as follows:

- We label our feature with a CR (or any other symbol that makes sense to our team), instead of a bug symbol.

- We describe the change requested (or link to it) in our feature's card details.

- We make any necessary modifications to our feature files.

> **Important note:**
>
> Be careful when analyzing CRs. Although some may seem to request changes to existing features, sometimes they will subtly lead to the creation of new features, or even capabilities. This is commonly known as **scope creep** or **feature creep** and can have negative consequences, so make sure you put any CRs thoroughly through the D3 process, so as to catch any potential extra features or capabilities that the CR necessitates.

We now know how to manage our development cycle using a feature-first methodology within Scrum. Let's take a look at how we can do the same using Kanban.

Working within Kanban

The Kanban method is another popular Agile approach. While Scrum is focused on an iterative and incremental development and delivery workflow, Kanban favors a more continuous flow. With Kanban, there are no required time-boxed events or iterations. System backlog cards are pulled into the **To do** columns as and when needed. There are some other things to note when working with Kanban:

- The **Doing** column has a card limit. Only a certain number of cards are allowed on it at any given time. This usually corresponds to the number of developers on the team, thus ensuring a developer is only working on one thing at any one time.

- The responsibility for managing the system backlog falls mainly to the **Service Request Manager** (**SRM**). This is an informal role similar to the Scrum's product owner, although the SRM is regarded more as a customer proxy, rather than someone who decides what the product should look and behave like.

- Kanban does not prescribe team roles such as Scrum master, product owner, and so on. Instead, individuals may be given the less formal roles of SRM and Service Delivery Manager. Other than that, everyone within the team has equal powers and responsibilities.

- In Scrum, any changes that violate the Sprint goal are prevented during the Sprint. Any out-of-Sprint changes need the approval of the product owner as well as the development team. In Kanban, any team member can add items to the task board at any time, as long as the **Doing** column limit is respected.

- Kanban does not prescribe a planning schedule or event. The team schedules planning meetings when it is deemed necessary.

- In Scrum, the task board is reset at the end of a Sprint. **Completed** and **Accepted** items are archived or moved. In Kanban, the board keeps constantly changing and evolving but never completely resets.

Overall, Kanban's continuous delivery approach simplifies the task board workflow. However, it makes the issue of planning code releases a bit more complicated. In Scrum, we release code at the end of the Sprint. Each release is tied to a Sprint goal or theme and releases are incremental, that is, they build on top of one another. This makes it easy to plan releases. For example, we may decide to release a beta version of our system at the end of Sprint 8. We then tag all code that has been released up to and including Sprint 8 as our beta release. We know, through the Sprint goals, what functionality and capabilities that release should deliver. Kanban's continuous – and seemingly random – delivery, however, means that release planning requires a little bit more consideration and effort. Fear not, though, as our feature-first approach makes our workflow much easier and risk-free.

Kanban planning

Although Kanban does not dictate formal planning meetings, it is advisable to have an informal planning session every 2 weeks or so. The activity and goal of this meeting should be similar to the Sprint Planning event, that is, to decide which features should be moved to the To do list. The criteria are almost the same as with Scrum:

1. **Priority**: Features are selected according to their priority, which is decided by the team in consultation with the Service Request Manager. The requirements model, with its hierarchical view of goals, capabilities, and features, should inform our decisions as to which features to prioritize.

2. **Fully-formedness**: Only features with full contextual information and detailed scenarios (as described in *Chapter 3, Writing Fantastic Features with the Gherkin Language*, in the *Writing a fully-formed feature* section), can be moved to the **To do** column.

3. **User Interface (UI) guidelines**: Many, if not most of our features will involve direct interaction with an actor through a UI. There are many ways in which the functionality implemented in a feature can be invoked by and presented to an actor. This is why it is very important that such features are accompanied by screen mock-ups or wireframes that allow us to aim for a specific UI layout and styling.

One thing we don't need to account for – that we do in Scrum – is load capacity, that is, estimating how many features we can work on within a Sprint (obviously, as there are no Sprints in Kanban). However, it is a good idea to limit how many features we place in the **To do** column. Having too many features there may suggest we are too hasty in our analysis. A limited number of To do features also helps focus the team and provide some scope for the upcoming work.

Kanban development cycle

As with Scrum, the aim is to move all features from the **To do** column to the **Accepted** column. The team will examine the features in the **To do** column and will come up with a set of tasks required to implement these features. These tasks are placed in the **Planning** column and the team follows the same workflow illustrated in *Fig. 7.2 – Sprint development workflow*. The only differences are depicted in the following diagram:

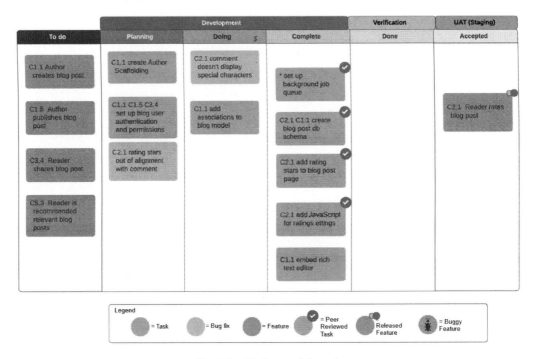

Fig. 7.8 – Kanban task board

Let's check what happened on the board:

1. The **Doing** column has a limit on it (5 in this example), which indicates the maximum number of items that can be on it at any one time.

2. When a feature has been pushed to staging and has been **Accepted**, it's simply labeled as *released*. Labeling features with release versions is done at the discretion of the team.

3. Once a task has been moved from the **Doing** column, we may drag another task for the same feature from the **Planning** column. If there are no other tasks for that feature, then we drag a task for a different feature.

Other than these, everything else flows the same way as with a Sprint development cycle. Of course, in Kanban, we don't have to worry about what to do at the beginning or end of the Sprint, as the Kanban development cycle is continuous and uninterrupted.

Dealing with change

In Kanban, changes can occur at any time. Unlike Scrum, we don't have to schedule the fixing of bugs or any requested changes for a specific iteration, that is, a Sprint. The two major kinds of change we'll have to deal with in our development cycle are emergent bugs and changes to existing features. We deal with both in a similar manner:

- We analyze and model any CRs following the methods detailed in *Chapter 5, Discovering and Analyzing Requirements*, in the *Discovering requirements* section.

- We label our feature with a CR or bug label, as appropriate.

- We describe the CR (or link to it) in our feature's card details.

- With a CR, we would almost certainly have to make changes to our feature's details, that is, in our feature files.

Overall, our task board workflow does not change dramatically between Scrum and Kanban. Scrum is great for regular and scoped software delivery. Kanban is more relaxed about delivery but tends to accommodate changes more easily.

Summary

In this chapter, we learned how to use the output of our requirements analysis and modeling process, that is, our features, to drive an agile development cycle using Scrum or Kanban. This is where the methods detailed in the previous chapters of this book start to pay big dividends. By knowing how to write features that are descriptive, robust, accurate, and finely scoped, we have ensured what we can use these features as complete, autonomous work units that can be completed within a Sprint. By having a requirements model that ties features to capabilities to stakeholder goals, we can easily classify and prioritize our features so we can address what our stakeholder needs most urgently and what adds the most value to them. By having step definitions for our features, that is, true executable specifications, we have an automated, consistent, and accurate way to measure when a feature is **done**.

We also learned how to apply JIT development with a feature-first approach. This approach cuts down waste and avoids the **user-story hell** phenomenon that plagues so many projects. We saw how this approach fits smoothly within the constraints of a Scrum or Kanban-based development cycle. In the next chapter, we will delve a little bit deeper into a short but essential part of our development process: verification. See you there!

6

8

Creating Automated Verification Code

In the preceding chapters, we learned how to create executable specifications, that is, features that can be automatically executed and verified. As stated previously, this book is not intended to make you an expert on writing automated verification. Much of such expertise relies on coding, and specific library and technology-related skills, so it falls outside this book's remit. Having said that, it would be remiss if a book on executable specifications and end-to-end delivery methodology did not give any advice on how to go about writing good automated verification code. In this chapter, we will learn how to architect and design our verification code by looking at the following:

- Why is automated verification valuable?
- Avoiding brittleness by layering automation code
- Leveraging automated verification code patterns

By the end of this chapter, you will know the basic principles behind writing solid, re-usable step definitions. You will also have a better understanding of the levels of abstraction involved while writing specifications and verification code.

Why is automated verification valuable?

There are two answers to this question. The first one should be easy to guess: because automated verification saves time and effort. We could verify our system's behavior by having someone sitting in front of a screen, running our system with one hand, while holding our specification with the other, and checking that everything works as we describe in our features. This approach will take a lot of that person's time and it runs the risk of that person getting tired or distracted and missing things or making mistakes. Alternatively, we could automatically run code that verifies our system consistently, reliably, and faster than a person can.

The second answer is much more appropriate. We have mentioned repeatedly throughout this book that features must reflect domain-level behavior, things that are important to an actor in the context of a particular feature's scenario. So, for instance, if our scenario for publishing a blog post has a *Given that the user is logged in as a Publisher* step, then this is a domain-level behavior. The actor involved in that scenario does not care how they logged in as a Publisher. They might have used a username and password, their fingerprint, their Twitter account, or something else. The verification code, that is, the step definition, is where we will interpret what *Logged in as a Publisher* means in terms of operational workflow or technical details. Knowing that this is the role of the verification code frees us from the mental shackles of having to think about these details when we write our domain behavior, that is, our scenarios. It reinforces the separation of concerns we must always follow when writing scenarios:

Scenario steps describe what happens in our system; step definitions describe how it happens and check that it does happen.

Separation of concerns is also extremely useful when writing step definitions. Let's see exactly why that is the case.

Avoiding brittleness by layering automation code

One of the most frequent reasons why some organizations don't write verification code (or start writing it and later give up) is that they find it difficult and time-consuming to maintain the step definitions. Every time something trivial changes on the UI or some other part of the code base, it triggers a wave of changes across our verification code. This is an understandable concern. Spending a lot of time and effort keeping our step definitions up to date is a self-defeating process. We call this kind of high-maintenance verification code **brittle**, as every little change tends to break it.

The brittle step definition problem

Let's look at how brittleness occurs in our verification code. Consider this scenario, saved under `features/ traveler_login.feature`:

```
Scenario: Successful log-in
Given Traveller is at the log-in page
When Traveller enters the correct username
And Traveller enters the correct password
And Traveller submits credentials
Then Traveller is taken to their bookings
And Traveller sees their booking
```

We could create a file, `features/step_definitions/ traveler_login.rb`, with our step definitions for this scenario as follows (using Ruby code with the `Watir` library):

```ruby
Given('Traveller is at the log-in page') do
    @browser.goto 'https://www.phptravels.net/login'
end


When('Traveller enters the correct username') do
    @browser.text_field(type: 'email').set 'user@phptravels.com'
end


When('Traveller enters the correct password') do
    @browser.text_field(type: 'password').set 'demouser'
end



When('Traveller submits credentials') do
    @browser.button(type: 'submit').click
    @browser.wait_until { @browser.window.url.include? 'https://
www.phptravels.net/account' }
end
```

```
Then('Traveller is taken to their bookings page') do
  assert_equal @browser.url, 'https://www.phptravels.net/
account/'
end


Then('Traveller sees their booking') do
  expected_hotel = 'Rendezvous Hotels'
  screen_hotel = @browser.element(css:  "#bookings > div.row
> div.col-md-5.offset-0.o4 > div.d-flex.flex-column > a > b
").text
  assert_equal screen_hotel, expected_hotel
end
```

This all looks fine, and a BDD tool like Cucumber will happily pick this step definition code up and run it. But let's look at the long-term prognosis. Our code relies too much on HTML element types and attributes. It looks for certain text fields with a specific name attribute value. It looks for a div element within a specific element ID. The thing is, HTML pages change constantly during a system's development. Each and every time we change the type or name attribute of our log-in credentials elements, our step definition will break. If we decide that our website will display the booking's hotel in a span element instead of a div element, for example, our step definition will break. Furthermore, any other step definitions that utilize the same elements will have to be changed too.

So, the way we have written the preceding step definitions results in brittleness. There are actions, however, that we can take to make our step definitions more solid and reduce the risk of brittleness.

Applying layers of abstraction

To shield our verification code from brittleness, we need to start viewing our verification process as consisting of distinct layers of abstraction, as depicted in the following diagram:

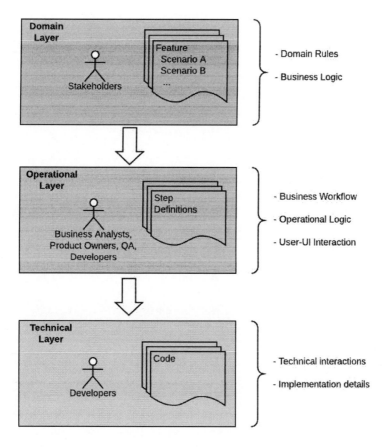

Fig. 8.1 – Layered design for change-resistant verification code

Let's break this diagram down and explain it:

- The **Domain Layer** is our specification, that is, our features. Our scenario steps use domain terminology that is understood by all stakeholders. They encapsulate our business logic, and our domain rules and constraints.

- The **Operational Layer** is our step definitions, that is, our verification code. We don't delve deep into technical or implementation details in our step definitions. Instead, we use code abstractions to capture the business workflow, the operations an actor undertakes to fulfill that step – the user journey, so to speak. In the next two sections, we'll discuss these code abstractions in detail. In-depth technical details should be avoided in this layer. Instead, they must be delegated to the Technical layer. Step definitions should be abstract enough so that technically-minded stakeholders, as well as developers, are able to understand them and even contribute to their writing. Ideally, step definition writing will involve developers, testers, business analysts, and other stakeholders.

- The **Technical Layer** is where our detailed, in-depth code lives. This is where we interact with HTML elements, databases, external services, and so on. This is where we worry about multi-threading, transaction locking, and all the other interesting programming challenges that programmers usually concern themselves with. We wouldn't expect anyone other than developers to be involved with this layer.

This layered approach, apart from providing a nice separation of concerns, also helps to mitigate the risk of changes and to reduce the brittleness of our code. The Domain layer will be the one least likely to change. The Technical layer is the one that will be changing most often, but we have now isolated the change impact to limited and specific points in our code base. So, if an HTML element changes its ID or attribute values, we won't have to change every single step definition that depends on that element. Instead, we will only need to change a single class or function within our Technical layer to apply the change. This has many benefits.

Consider, for instance, that we need to verify that a particular UI-dependent feature runs successfully on small-screen devices, such as cell phones. We already have the verification code for this feature that verifies the feature's behavior on a desktop-based UI layout. However, that verification code fails when run on a small-screen device. The reason for that failure is that the UI layout and user interaction on small screens is different to that on a desktop, so some HTML elements may not be accessible without scrolling, and some actions may rely on gestures instead of key presses. Using a layered approach, we won't have to create a new set of step definitions for our small-screen code verification. The operational workflow, which is reflected in the step definitions, doesn't change for small-screen devices, so our step definitions remain intact. All we have to do is add another Technical layer set of classes or functions for the small-screen implementation of our step definitions.

Let's look at a couple of useful patterns we can use to apply this layered approach to our verification code.

Leveraging automated verification code patterns

Just like with any other code, we can apply standard code patterns to our verification code in order to improve our code's structure or maintainability. As detailed in the previous sections of this chapter, we can minimize our verification code's brittleness by having our step definition code reflect an operational level of knowledge, rather than the nitty-gritty technical details. We will achieve that by using two tried and tested code patterns, the Page Object and the Façade. Let's look at the Page Object first.

Hiding browser details with the Page Object pattern

The Page Object pattern is a way to represent HTML pages and their elements in reusable classes. Page Objects provide an abstraction that allows us to write browser-interaction code that is reusable and maintainable. It works like this:

1. We create a Page Object for each web page our operational workflow uses. The object has methods that represent the interactions available on a given page. It encapsulates all the technical details needed in order to successfully interact with a web page. Our step definitions use the Page Object abstraction and never have to worry about browser or HTML element details.

2. Let's use the code we used in the *The brittle step definition problem* section, as a case in point. The original step definition code was as follows (I am omitting the Given/When/Then clauses for brevity and clarity):

```ruby
@browser.goto 'https://www.phptravels.net/login'
@browser.text_field(type: 'email').set 'user@phptravels.com'
@browser.text_field(type: 'password').set 'demouser'
@browser.button(type: 'submit').click
@browser.wait_until { @browser.window.url.include? 'https://www.phptravels.net/account' }
assert_equal @browser.url, 'https://www.phptravels.net/account/'
expected_hotel = 'Rendezvous Hotels'
screen_hotel = @browser.element(css:  "#bookings > div.row > div.col-md-5.offset-0.o4 > div.d-flex.flex-column > a > b ").text
assert_equal screen_hotel, expected_hotel
```

3. Now, we want to hide all HTML element access and other technical details. So, let's create some classes that do just that:

```ruby
class Container
  def initialize(browser)
    @browser = browser
  end
end

class Website < Container
```

```
    def login_page
      @login_page = LoginPage.new(@browser)
    end

    def booking_page
      @booking_page = BookingPage.new(@browser)
    end

    def close
      @browser.close
    end
  end
```

The `Container` class is just a root class that provides the `initializer` method to instantiate a `browser` object. The `Website` class encapsulates the layout of a website. The two methods, `login_page` and `booking_page`, are responsible for taking us to the pages that we want to interact with, by delegating to the respective objects. When we are finished, we call `close` to close our browser.

4. Let's implement the `LoginPage` class:

```
class LoginPage < Container
    URL = https://www.phptravels.net/login

    def open
      @browser.goto URL
      self
    end

    def login_as(user, pass)
      user_field.set user
      password_field.set pass
      login_button.click

      next_page = BookingPage.new(@browser)
      Watir::Wait.until { next_page.loaded? }
      next_page
```

```
        end

    private
    def user_field
        @browser.text_field(type: 'email')
    end

    def password_field
        @browser.text_field(type: 'password')
    end

    def login_button
        @browser.button(type: 'submit')
    end
  end
```

The `LoginPage` class is responsible for authorizing us to access the website with the `login_as` method. In a similar manner, we would also build a `BookingPage` class that would be responsible for doing whatever booking-related things we needed to do.

5. We have now hidden all HTML and other implementation details within methods for the website, and the `LoginPage` and `UserPage` classes. We can now write our step definitions as follows (omitting the `Given/When/Then` clauses for brevity):

```
@site = Website.new(Watir::Browser.new)
@login_page = @site.login_page.open
@booking_page = @login_page.login_as 'user@phptravels.
com', 'demouser'
assert @booking_page
assert @booking_page.booked_in?
@site.close
```

As you can see, our step definition code now refers to websites, login pages, and booking pages, instead of element types, attributes, and IDs. We now have an Operational layer encapsulation that doesn't need to worry about technical details. Most of our stakeholders should be able to read this code and understand what's going on. If our HTML changes, our step definitions remain valid. The Page Object pattern is a very useful device for hiding browser and HTML details from our step definitions.

Wrap up complex operations with the Façade Pattern

The Page Object pattern nicely encapsulates web page interactivity. Sometimes, however, we want to focus on how the user interacts with the system, rather than how the system interacts with the user. We want to encapsulate interactivity from the user's point of view, rather than the point of view of a web page. We can shift the perspective by using the Façade pattern.

The Façade is a software design pattern commonly used in object-oriented programming. A Façade is an object or component that serves as a front-facing interface masking more complex underlying or structural code.

A Façade helps hide unnecessary browser and other technical details from our step definitions and offer different entry points to underlying subsystems. We can write a Façade for our logging-in step definition. The Façade will encapsulate all intended operations of a `Traveller` user:

```ruby
class Traveller
  def initialize
    @browser = Watir::Browser.new
  end

  def visit(url)
    @browser.goto url
  end

  def login(usr, pwd, confirmation_page)
    @browser.text_field(type: 'email').set usr
    @browser.text_field(type: 'password').set pwd
    @browser.button(type: 'submit').click
    @browser.wait_until { @browser.window.url.include?
confirmation_page}
  end

  def find_booking
    @browser.element(css:   "#bookings > div.row > div.col-md-5.
offset-0.o4 > div.d-flex.flex-column > a > b ")
  end

  def logged_in?
```

```
        @browser.div(id:   "logged-in ")
    end
end
```

The `log_in` method will take us to the website and log us in. The `find_booking` method will find the HTML element containing the booking info. Every other behavior we need to enact, as a `Traveller`, will be implemented as a method within our `Traveller` class.

We can now write our step definition as follows (the `Given/When/Then` clauses have been omitted for brevity):

```
@traveller.visit( "https://www.phptravels.net/login ")
@traveller.login( "user@phptravels.com' ",   "demouser ",
"https://www.phptravels.net/account/ ")
assert @traveller.logged_in?
@traveller.visit('https://www.phptravels.net/account/')
booking = @traveller.find_booking
assert booking.text, 'Rendezvous Hotels'
```

The value of a Façade is that it enables the hiding of complex interactions within simple methods. For instance, the `find_booking` method knows how to find the hotel name hidden within a booking HTML element. If our booking page's design or implementation is changed, so that the hotel name is located elsewhere, our step definitions will still be calling the same `find_booking` method and they will, therefore, be unaffected.

Knowing which patterns to apply and when to apply them

Both the Page Object and Façade patterns can be very useful, so how can we tell which one to use? The key here is understanding the context of these patterns. The Page Object pattern encapsulates the interactions on specific web pages. This works very well when the steps we are verifying involve single web pages, such as logging in or listing bookings. However, some steps may involve more complex interactions; this is particularly true of *Given* steps, which set initial conditions. For example, we may see steps like *Given a traveller has made a booking*, which would involve a special workflow or user journey. This would usually involve a set of distinct operations such as logging in, finding a holiday, booking it, paying for it, and so on. It would necessitate navigation between multiple web pages. In such a case, a `Traveller` façade with a `book_holiday` method would prove invaluable. This method would abstract all the necessary operations needed to make a booking and could be repeated as and when necessary.

In fact, a common practice is to use both Page Object and Façade patterns together. So, our `Traveller` façade's `book_holiday` method's implementation could leverage Page Objects to abstract interactions with specific web pages. This double whammy approach provides abstraction at both the web page and the user-journey level.

Separating the things we verify from the way we verify them

We saw how the Page Object and Façade patterns can be used to separate implementation details from operational details. Let's revisit our previous diagram and see how everything fits together:

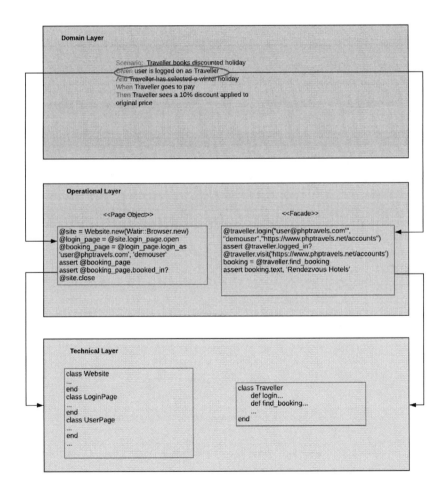

Fig. 8.2 – Layered interactions separate Domain, Operational, and Technical logic

As depicted in the preceding diagram, our feature scenario has a *Given user is logged in as a Traveller* step. Our scenarios describe domain actions and they live in the Domain layer. Our *log in* step can be verified by running a step definition, that is, some code that makes sure that the user is logged in as a `Traveller`.

Our step definitions don't know how our system is implemented or how our web pages are designed, but they know what the business workflow should be like – they know which operations need to be performed to log a user in as a Traveller. They can either perform these operations from the perspective of the UI (the Page Object pattern) or from the user's perspective (the Façade pattern). These operations simply delegate to some code that knows how our system works, that is, which HTML elements capture the password, which elements contain the booking, and so on.

By leveraging this multi-layered approach, we are making our verification process much more resistant to brittleness, as we separate the behavior we verify (for instance, `@traveller.find_booking`) from the details of how we verify it (`browser. element(css:   "#bookings > div.row > div.col-md-5.offset-0.o4 > div.d-flex.flex-column > a > b ")`).

Summary

In this chapter, we examined one of the main obstacles with end-to-end BDD adoption: the fragility of verification code. We discussed how a multi-layer architecture, realized with two handy design patterns (Page Object and Façade), and can reduce step definition brittleness and decrease the maintenance cost of our verification code. But another great benefit is that knowing how to write good, solid step definitions will make you better at writing features. Understanding why we need to abstract the Domain, Operational, and Technical layers and how they interact with each other will give you a much deeper insight into BDD, will make it easier to distinguish and capture Domain behaviors, and will ultimately make you a better system builder.

This chapter brings to an end the instructive part of this book. In the next chapter, we'll take a look at everything we've learned so far, bringing it all together under the umbrella of the canonical requirements life cycle.

9
The Requirements Life Cycle

In the last few chapters of this book, we have been delving into the nitty-gritty details of system backlogs, task boards, the development life cycle, and verification code. In this chapter, we'll take a high-level view of what we have learned so far. This includes looking at how it all fits together as an integrated, working, Agile methodology within the context of the requirements life cycle stages. In detail, we will be covering the following topics:

- Revisiting the requirements life cycle
- Applying the Agile requirements management workflow

By the end of this chapter, you will know how the different techniques and methods presented in this book fit within the canonical requirements management life cycle model. You will also better understand how they all flow together in a continuous, delineated, end-to-end methodology that enables us to convert raw requirements into working code.

Mapping the different stages of the requirements life cycle against relevant and pragmatic methods or techniques will give you a more holistic understanding of how these methods help with requirements management. This will also solidify the lessons of this book. Knowing how you can use these methods to elicit diverse requirements from our stakeholders, analyze them, model them, convert them to verifiable specifications, and deliver them in an agile manner, will cement your ability to manage building the correct software. This will ultimately help you deliver the system that your stakeholders want and deserve.

Revisiting the requirements management life cycle

In *Chapter 1, The Requirements Domain*, we talked about the requirements management life cycle, where I claimed that this book would provide methods and techniques that will help you implement every stage of it. It is now time to back this claim up and discuss how what you've learned in this book can be applied to each and every stage of the requirements life cycle. We shall illustrate this with an example project regarding a knowledge-sharing website. The initial requirements for this system are summarized as follows:

- Knowledge producers (authors, in this case) can share their knowledge as blog posts, recorded videos, or live sessions.

- Shared content will either be free or premium. Premium content can be purchased for a fee.

- Authors decide which content is free and which is premium, as well as the fee for premium content.

- A percentage of the fees that have been paid for premium content go to the website owners. The rest goes to the authors.

- Knowledge consumers can search for content based on topics, tags, or producers' names.

- Content must be able to be consumed on a diverse range of desktop and mobile devices.

Now, let's examine how our methodology fits within the requirements management life cycle, one stage at a time, by providing examples.

Validating requirements

Validation is about ensuring that the requirements fulfil a realistic and useful business need. Our methodology ensures that everything is traced back to a goal, so we immediately know the business need fulfilled by any given task we are working on. In *Chapter 1, The Requirements Domain*, in the *Identifying goals* section, we also examined how to validate business and domain goals in order to establish that they reflect realistic and useful business needs.

Example: The business makes it clear that content should be available on a number of different devices. We identify a list of devices and browsers that we intend to support. One of the business's account managers wants us to add support for the Internet Explorer browser since a client whose account he looks after is still using that browser. This seems like a reasonable requirement but doing some quick market research tells us that Internet Explorer's share is 6% and dropping. We already know from *Chapter 1, The Requirements Domain*, that a requirement must be ultimately tied to a goal that either increases and protects revenue or reduces and avoids costs. Supporting Internet Explorer will give us a potentially small increase in revenue and cost a large amount of money for supporting and maintaining compatibility with that browser. Overall, the business need for this requirement appears to be neither realistic nor useful to anyone apart from the director's personal reputation with a specific client.

Modeling requirements

Modeling is about having a structured and consistent way to describe and store requirements. We are doing exactly that by using Impact Mapping as our modeling tool and by having clear and precise definitions of the entities in our requirements model, as described in *Chapter 1, The Requirements Domain*, and *Chapter 2, Impact Mapping and Behavior-Driven Development*. Also, in *Chapter 5, Discovering and Analyzing Requirements*, we set out clear rules about how to define and derive those entities.

Example: In our knowledge-sharing website example, after applying the techniques from *Chapter 5, Discovering and Analyzing Requirements*, we'll end up with a standard requirements model. It will look something like the following diagram (displaying only a small part of the model for illustration purposes):

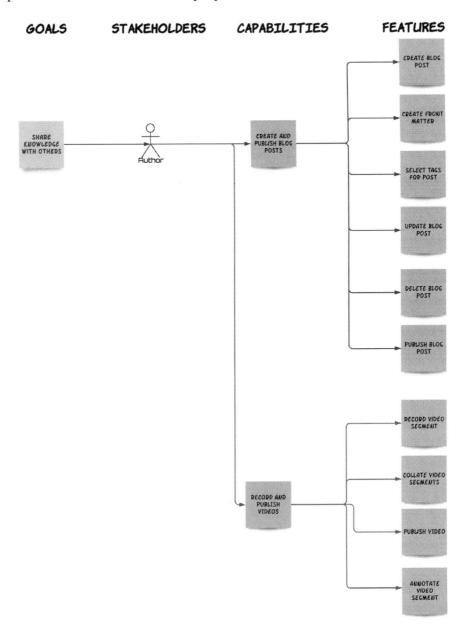

Fig. 9.1 – Example requirements model

Every requirements model has the same structure and contains the same type of entities. It therefore provides a structured and consistent way of modeling requirements.

Creating specifications

The specification stage is one of the most important ones as without a specification, we cannot deliver the correct system. This stage is where we translate the requirements into concrete and clear system behaviors; that is, our features. In *Chapter 3, Writing Fantastic Features with the Gherkin Language*, and *Chapter 4, Crafting Features Using Principles and Patterns*, we discussed how to write such concrete and clear system behaviors extensively. In *Chapter 5, Discovering and Analyzing Requirements*, we learned how to translate requirements into goals, capabilities, and features. One of this book's central themes is bridging the gap between requirements and specifications, which we do by applying the right analysis techniques (refer to *Chapter 5, Discovering and Analyzing Requirements*) and creating a hierarchical, delineated requirements model (*Chapter 2, Impact Mapping and Behavior-Driven Development*).

Example: We can pick an identified feature from our requirements model and specify its behavior in a feature file, which will look something like the following:

```
Feature: Author updates blog post
User Story: As an Author, I want to update a blog post,
so that I can correct any mistakes or inaccuracies
Impact: http://example.com/my-project/impacts-map


Background:
Given the user is logged in as an Author
And the Author goes to their Blog Posts
And the Author selects the "How to reduce memory footprint"
blog post
And the Author chooses to edit the post


Scenario Outline: Successful word editing
When the Author moves into the editor part of the page
And the Author replaces the words <existing> word with the
<new> word
And the Author saves the blog post
And the Author views the "How to reduce memory footprint" blog
post
```

```
Then the Autor cannot see the <existing> words


Examples:
 | existing | new |
 | 100 | 1000 |
 | ommit | omit |
```

`Feature` prescribes a clear system behavior that our development team can take away and implement as system code. We should also share our features with our stakeholders in a specification document.

Classifying requirements

Requirements can be classified according to the area of the system they affect, their complexity level, their risk level, and many other factors. The guide to the **Business Analysis Body of Knowledge (BABOK** – `https://www.iiba.org/standards-and-resources/babok/`) describes four types of requirements:

- **Business requirements** represent business objectives. These are our business and domain goals, as represented on the first level of the requirements model.

- **Stakeholders requirements** represent the requirements of individual stakeholders. They reflect the impact stakeholders need to have on our system in their quest to accomplish their goals. These are our capabilities and they comprise the second level of the requirements model.

- **Solution requirements** represent the requirements of a solution. These requirements form the basis on which the development team will develop the system. They are our features and they occupy the third level of the requirements model.

- **Transition requirements** are temporary requirements that are needed to facilitate a solution and they usually relate to data migration, data cleaning, or user training. In reality, no requirement is really transient as every requirement leaves a residue of value behind after it's fulfilled. So, transition requirements will be captured in the usual form of goal – capability – feature in our requirements model. For instance, we may have a *Migrate data from legacy system* capability, with a related *Administrator batch imports user from old system* feature. Although this feature may be executed only once, it will affect our system during its lifetime, so it must be dealt with like any other required behavior.

So, in summary, the methodology presented in this book provides us with an already structured and classified requirements model that is in line with industry standards.

Example: The requirements model for our *knowledge-sharing site example* (*Figure 9.1*) already presents the captured requirements, which are visually classified as follows:

- **Business Requirements**: Our customers can share knowledge with others.

- **Stakeholder Requirements**: Create and publish blog posts, record and publish videos.

- **Solution Requirements**: Create blog post, create front matter, tag post, record video segment, and many others.

Classifying requirements helps us understand and further process the requirements model well.

Documenting requirements

One of the great things about writing features with Gherkin is that features are self-documented. Using a simple, ubiquitous language that anyone can understand means that our system's behavior can easily by perceived simply by reading these features. Our requirements model also serves as a visual guide to our requirements, providing a classified and traceable tree of our analysis outcome. Furthermore, in *Chapter 6, Organizing Requirements*, in the *Creating a Specification document* section, we detailed the creation of a specifications document, which provides accumulated, annotated, and comprehensive documentation for our system. Providing ample and accessible requirements documentation is one of the greatest benefits our methodology offers.

Example: The *Author updates blog post* feature, which we created earlier in this chapter, describes in a non-technical, domain-specific language the system behavior for that particular functionality in a step-by-step manner. It can be easily read by businesspeople, as well as developers.

Prioritizing requirements

There are four general approaches to prioritizing requirements:

- **By value**: This is about the benefits a requirement gives to stakeholders. These could be of business or economic value. It is common to prioritize higher-value requirements first. Because our requirements model associates stakeholders with goals and capabilities, it is easy to select the stakeholders we want to please the most and choose the most high-value capabilities these stakeholders need. We can then drill down to each capability's feature and decide which ones to implement first.

- **By cost**: Cost prioritizing can be about implementing the requirements that need the least time, effort, or money first (the *low-hanging fruit* approach). It can also be about implementing requirements with the greatest **return on investment (ROI)**. Our requirements model makes it easier to discern both cost and ROI. By following the methodology in this book – *Chapter 3, Writing Fantastic Features with the Gherkin Language,* and *Chapter 4, Crafting Features Using Principles and Patterns,* in particular – we should have a set of well-scoped features associated with each capability. This means that we shouldn't have to break down any features even further and that no one feature should take an extraordinary amount of time to implement. This is no replacement for proper estimation, but it should enable a relative, ball-park assessment of a capability's cost, simply based on the number of features required to deliver it. Also, since a capability is tied to a goal, we should be able to get a feel for the potential return of our cost investment. Business goals are always underlined by financial motives, such as increasing profit or protecting from losses, so these are the goals with the potentially highest ROI.

- **By risk**: Prioritizing based on risk is most commonly used on projects in new, controversial, or disruptive areas. The idea is that if the high-risk requirements fail to be delivered, then the project can be scaled down or even abandoned. Being able to trace a feature to a capability, and then to a goal, on our requirements model makes it easier to appreciate the inherent business risk of a feature we plan to implement. This should always be complemented by an assessment of the technical risk associated with the feature.

- **By urgency**: Some requirements are more time-sensitive than others. For instance, our client may need to demonstrate some capability at a trade show or exhibition.

Regardless of the prioritization method used, our requirements model's visual nature and hierarchical structure makes it much easier to prioritize requirements than the usual text-based methods.

Example: In our *knowledge sharing* example, we identified three capabilities that will help the *author stakeholder* achieve their goal. Let's suppose that the fee that's charged for having interactive sessions will be higher than the fee for watching video content, which will, in turn, be higher than the fee for reading blog posts. We can then prioritize these capabilities in terms of economic value, where *Arrange Interactive Session* will have the highest priority and *Create and Publish Post* will have the lowest one.

Now, let's suppose that the *Arrange Interactive Session* capability has 20 features associated with it (trust me, it takes a lot of functionalities to arrange online sessions). Let's also assume that we followed the advice given in *Chapter 4, Crafting Features Using Principles and Patterns*, by breaking down composite or CRUD features. We could then reasonably assume that *Arrange Interactive Session* was more costly than *Create and Publish Post* (which has six features). So, if we prioritized by cost, *Create and Publish Post* would have a higher priority than *Arrange Interactive Session*.

The structure, hierarchy, and visual simplicity of our requirements model makes classifying requirements much easier and less stressful.

Verifying requirements

Verification is about ensuring that our system functions in a way that fulfills our requirements. Because our analysis methodology results in executable specifications, we have an out-of-the-box way of verifying our system, as explained in *Chapter 3, Writing Fantastic Features with the Gherkin Language*, in the *Features are executable specifications* section. By using a BDD tool and the right approach to writing verification code (as detailed in *Chapter 8, Automating Verification*), we can ensure that we have an automated way of verifying our features. Since each feature is tied to a capability and, from there, to a stakeholder and goal, verified features equate to fulfilled stakeholder goals; that is, fully verified requirements.

Example: In the *Creating specifications* section, earlier in this chapter, we created a specification for the *Author updates blog post* Feature. To verify that feature, we would also have written some step definition code that executes the conditions specified in the **Given** steps, the actions in the **When** steps, and asserted that the outcomes in the **Then** steps did actually occur. We would then be reassured that our system does indeed behave the way we specified it would.

Dealing with change

This is about dealing with changes to requirements. How we achieve that relies largely on the delivery cycle we adopt. An incremental and iterative delivery cycle such as the one prescribed by the Scrum framework requires a slightly different approach to a continuous delivery cycle, such as the one prescribed by the Kanban method. Change management techniques for both of these cycles were detailed in *Chapter 7, Feature-First Development*. To summarize, the key things to apply in order to be change-resilient are as follows:

- **Feature-First development**: By focusing our development and delivery on the things that are constant (features), rather than transient (development tasks, bug fixes, and so on), we can isolate and discern what changes from how it changes and, therefore, deal with it more effectively.

- **Tracked delivery**: By keeping track of when features are deployed or delivered, such as sprint numbers or release versions, we can easily track changes and their effects on both our system behavior and the underlying code.

Let's examine this within the scope of our current example.

Example: Let's suppose we are developing our knowledge sharing system within Scrum. At the end of our first sprint, we have delivered two features: BL.1 and BL.2. Our Scrum Board will look as follows:

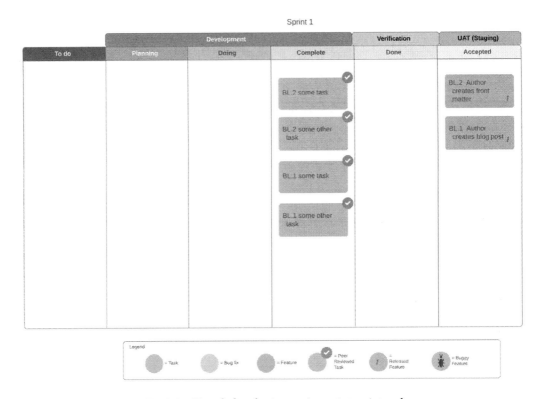

Fig. 9.2 – Knowledge sharing project – 1st sprint end

Our BL.1 and BL.2 features are labelled with the 1 (for 1st sprint) tag. Now, let's imagine that our stakeholders require a change in the behavior of BL.1. We need to add some new Steps or Scenarios to our Feature and drag the board card for BL.1 back into the sprint backlog (**To do** list) for the next sprint.

Let's also imagine that a small defect was discovered with our delivered BL.2 feature. It will have to be fixed, so we drag the board card for BL.2 back into the sprint backlog too.

When Sprint 2 starts, we create a task to implement the changes in BL.1 and a task to correct the defect in BL.2. Our Scrum board for Sprint 2 looks as follows:

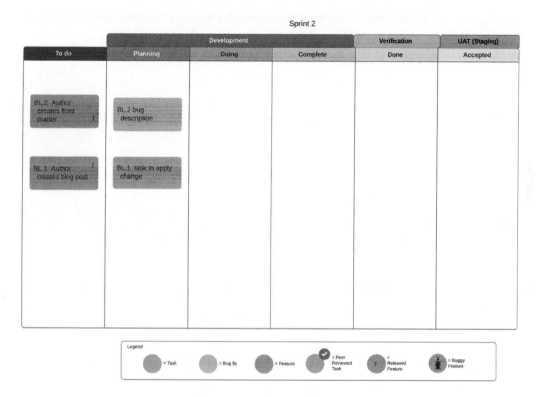

Fig. 9.3 – Knowledge sharing project – 2nd sprint start

At the end of the Sprint, when our tasks are complete and our Features have been verified and accepted, we label the features as 2 (meaning they're released with the 2nd sprint). Our Scrum Board now looks as follows:

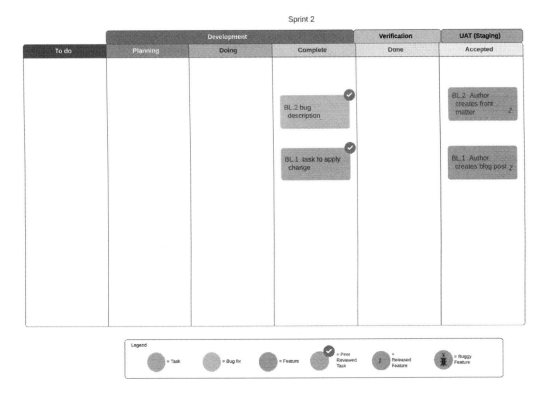

Fig. 9.4 – Knowledge sharing project – 2nd sprint end

By tracking and labelling feature releases, we can see how and when our features change over time. By including the feature release labels in our source version control system (git, for instance), we have an audit trail of our system changes, as well as the related code changes.

One of the biggest benefits of our requirements analysis and modeling methodology is that it ties in seamlessly with a Feature-First delivery and development cycle. This means that changes are analyzed and modeled like any other requirements, and that our system backlog and task board reflect these changes without clutter and ambiguity.

It's now time to look at how the methods and techniques displayed in this section come together in an integrated workflow.

Applying the Agile requirements management workflow

Throughout this book, we've learned about different techniques, processes, and methods for dealing with various stages of the analysis and development life cycle. We can now put them all together in an integrated workflow that will start by capturing raw requirements from the stakeholders and end by delivering working code that verifiably delivers what our stakeholders require.

Our workflow consists of four distinct phases:

1. Elicitation and Analysis

2. Discovery and Modeling

3. Executable Specification

4. Development and Verification

These phases will be repeated time and time again throughout our project's life cycle, for each set of requirements that comes to our attention and through each development cycle or iteration (**sprint**). They will also be applied concurrently, where some of our team members will be eliciting requirements from the stakeholders, while some other team members will be creating `Scenarios` for discovered `Features`, and someone else will be writing code to implement the most high-priority `Features` on our task board. Let's look at each phase more closely.

Elicitation and Analysis

When our project is about to start and throughout its development, requirements will be thrown at us from different directions and in different forms, such as conversational, textual, diagrammatic, or formal. Often, we will have to draw requirements out of stakeholders, deduce them from existing documentation, or infer them from a legacy system's behavior. The **Elicitation and Analysis** phase aims to draw out requirements from the stakeholders in a clear and specific manner, which will then allow us to map the raw requirements to well-defined and fine-scoped requirement domain entities; that is, goals, stakeholders, capabilities, and features, as described in *Chapter 1, The Requirements Domain*, and *Chapter 2, Impact Mapping and Behavior-Driven Development*.

The mental model we use during this phase is that of a separation funnel, as depicted in the following diagram:

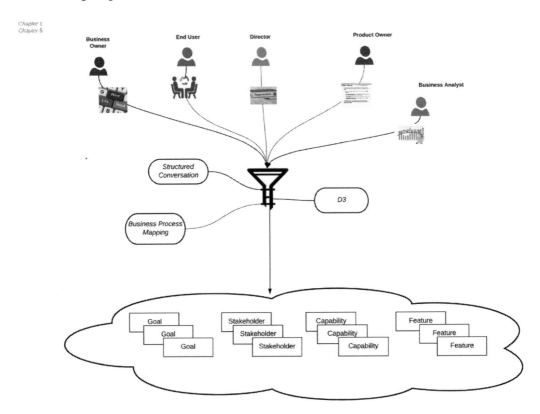

Fig. 9.5 – The Elicitation and Analysis phase

Raw requirements come into the funnel from different sources and in different forms. We apply filtering techniques in order to separate values from waste and identify the requirement domain entities that these raw requirements encapsulate. These filtering techniques are Structured Conversation, D3, and Business Process Mapping, as explained in *Chapter 5, Discovering and Analyzing Requirements*. The outcome of this phase is a number of entities, such as goals, stakeholder, capabilities, and features.

Modeling and Discovery

The aim of this phase is to produce a requirements model using the entities identified in the Elicitation and Analysis phase. The requirements model is a tree-like structure that visually displays our requirement domain entities and their associations, as depicted in the following diagram:

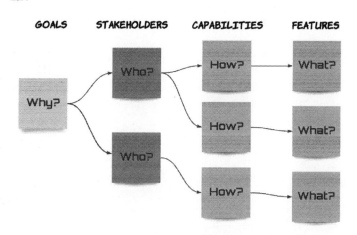

Fig. 9.6 – The Modeling and Discovery phase

The requirements model provides quick and easy traceability so that any team member can trace a feature to a capability, stakeholder, and goal. Not only does the requirements model ensure that everyone can see the big picture, but it also allows us to get proactive. Having a visual and hierarchical representation of the requirements, as discussed in *Chapter 2, Impact Mapping and Behavior-Driven Development*, makes it easier to discover new requirements or functionality. For instance, by knowing the goal that a capability helps accomplish, we may come up with new capabilities to accomplish the same goal. Similarly, knowing a capability, in the context of its relevant stakeholder and goals, enables us to discover the right functionality (features) needed to deliver the capability correctly. The requirements model is a uniquely valuable artifact and is at the heart of the methodology presented in this book.

Executable specification

Here, in the last level of our requirements model, our features form the input for the next phase. The executable specification phase is crucial to the successful delivery of our system. Our specifications are our fully-formed features; that is, our features are fleshed out with scenarios written in a ubiquitous language that's easily understood by our stakeholders. These features are stored in feature (`.feature`) files and they are the basis on which code development will proceed. Together with the system glossary, the stakeholder model, and other contextual information, they form the specifications document, which we can deliver to our stakeholders, as illustrated in the following diagram:

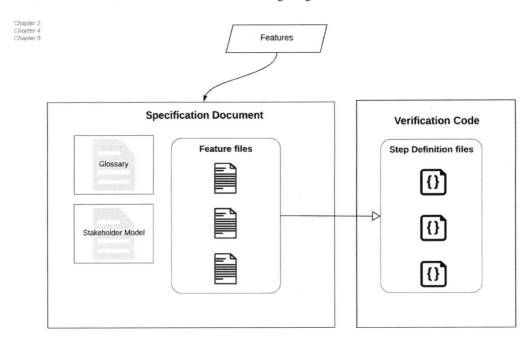

Fig. 9.7 – Executable specification

The specification document should contain everything the stakeholders need to know about our system. *Chapter 3, Writing Fantastic Features with the Gherkin Language,* and *Chapter 4, Crafting Features Using Principles and Patterns,* explain in great detail how to write features correctly.

In addition to fully describing our system's behavior, these features can also be executed; that is, they can be verified against our delivered system. We achieve this by creating step definitions; that is, verification code that matches the steps described in our feature scenarios with actions on our system's interface. *Chapter 8, Automating Verification,* details how to write solid step definitions. By having comprehensive features and matching step definitions to verify them, we have ourselves a truly executable specification.

Development, Validation, and Verification

No requirements management methodology would be useful if it didn't explain how to turn requirements into working and verified code. The fully-formed features that are created at the executable specification phase form the cornerstone of our development process. Our **Feature-First approach** means that our system backlog consists entirely of features. Our job, as system builders, ultimately comes down to that: implementing features. To do that, we will need to complete certain tasks, which we store and monitor under the Development column of our task board. Tasks are transient; we only do them in order to implement a feature. Once all feature tasks are complete, we can verify our feature by using a BDD tool to run our step definitions against a version of the system that includes that feature, as depicted in the following diagram:

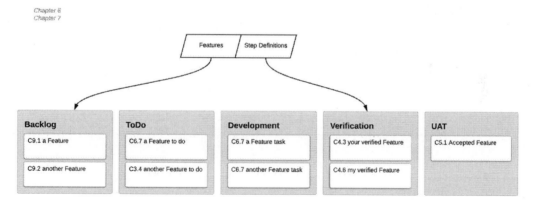

Fig. 9.8 – Development, Validation, and Verification

Once verification is successful, we can deploy the feature on a staging server and get our users to validate the features and give us their feedback. *Chapter 6, Organizing Requirements,* and *Chapter 7, Feature-First Development,* go into great depth in order to explain this process, also taking into account different Agile development and delivery approaches.

Summary

This chapter brought together the techniques, methods, and processes we've examined so far in this book. A comprehensive requirements management methodology should address all the stages of the traditional life cycle. In the first section of this chapter, we explained how each requirements management stage was dealt with in this book. In the second section, we iterated how each lesson of this book can be brought together in an integrated workflow that allows us to start with raw requirements and end up with verified and working code, which is the main purpose of this book.

This chapter recapped, summarized, and enhanced everything we've learned about in this book. This should help you understand how different techniques and methods flow together in an integrated methodology that enables us to deliver working code from raw requirements.

In previous chapters, we addressed individual chunks of the requirements management puzzle. In this chapter, we took a step back and looked at the whole puzzle as one big, beautiful picture. By looking at the big picture we can better appreciate the importance of the individual pieces and how well they fit together in order to provide the desired outcome.

In the next chapter, we'll look at how to apply the first stages of our workflow to a fictional, yet realistic, use case. Stay tuned for the Camford University paper publishing system!

Further reading

- Kent J. McDonald, *Beyond Requirements: Analysis with an Agile Mindset*, Addison-Wesley Professional; 1st edition (29 Aug. 2015)

- Dean Leffingwell, *Agile Software Requirements: Lean Requirements Practices for Teams, Programs, and the Enterprise*, Addison Wesley; 1 edition (27 Dec. 2010)

- Dan Olsen, *The Lean Product Playbook: How to Innovate with Minimum Viable Products and Rapid Customer Feedback*, Wiley; 1st edition (June 2, 2015)

10

Use Case: The Camford University Paper Publishing System

In previous chapters of this book, we learned how to manage requirements in order to provide a successful software delivery. In this, the final chapter, we will examine how our knowledge can be applied to a real-life use case. Camford University is obviously not real, but the nature of the requirements, interactions, and events described herein are all based on actual cases that I've encountered in my career in the course of various projects. In particular, we will learn about the following:

- Understanding the Camford conundrum
- Eliciting requirements
- Analyzing requirements
- Planning the way forward

This chapter intends to give some context to all the knowledge imparted in this book. You will get a taste of how to apply all the requirement elicitation and specification methods you've learned in this book to a new project. You will also learn how to conduct two important project milestones: the first two client-side meetings.

Understanding the Camford conundrum

Our fictional Camford University is one of the oldest and most reputable universities in the country. As a worldwide center of excellence, they are renowned for their high-quality teaching and innovative research. They publish hundreds of academic papers each year, via their publishing department, Camford Press. They have been publishing ground-breaking papers for centuries, which is where the conundrum lies. Their methods of publishing haven't changed much in the last few decades, which is now causing them a problem as they find it difficult to cope with the increasing supply of papers by an ever-expanding university. Although Camford Press has unparalleled knowledge and skills in the academic peer review and publishing processes, they are not really up to speed with modern technologies and they do not fully comprehend how to leverage such technologies to their benefit. They did upgrade their process to an email-based system a few years back, but they are now looking to move into the 21st century, technologically speaking.

This is why Camford Press has now turned to our organization with an overarching remit:

To automate and improve our peer review process

During our initial communications, they highlighted the main areas they want to address:

- Reduce the time to check whether submitted papers adhere to the University's publishing guidelines. They currently have to do a visual check of each submitted paper, which takes a lot of time and effort.

- Reduce the time it takes to provide feedback to authors. This is currently done by exchanging emails with attached documents.

- Make it easier to find and notify paper reviewers. Right now, they have a written list of reviewers, whom they contact by letter, telephone, or email in order to ask them if they can peer review a paper.

- Create a secure way to transfer and review academic papers. The reliance on email has caused some papers to be sent to the wrong recipients, by accident, and even had some emails intercepted by man-in-the-middle attacks. This resulted in the leakage of confidential and commercially sensitive information, which has caused a great deal of embarrassment to the University.

This is the outline of Camford Press's requirements. We have arranged a meeting with the major stakeholders in order to get more details and increase our understanding of what exactly they need. So, let's attend our first meeting and meet our stakeholders.

Eliciting requirements

At our first meeting with our client stakeholders, our objectives are fairly simple:

1. Get to know the stakeholders and their role in the process we are implementing

2. Obtain a basic understanding of the stakeholders' expectations

3. Understand the stakeholders' goals and identify which capabilities we need to deliver in order to help them realize their goals

It is important that we keep conversations focused and targeted toward identifying requirement domain entities. It's also important that we validate their goals, so as to avoid any unrealistic or vanity goals that may derail the project.

Leading the initial discussions

When we arrive at the offices of Camford Press, we are introduced to the following people:

- Professor Priya Chakrabarti, the editor-in-chief of Camford Press

- Dr. Elizabeth Braddock, Camford University's IS manager

We are also informed that we should have met Dr. Tom Logan, Camford Press' Managing Editor, but he is currently on an international flight and he will be away for the next 2 weeks.

Following the preparatory small talk and cups of coffee, we get down to business and have a structured conversation with the stakeholders.

The Editor-in-Chief (EiC) interview

Us: So, Professor Chakrabarti, could you please tell us what your role in Camford Press involves?

EiC: I have oversight of the whole review and publication process. It is my responsibility to ensure that everything runs smoothly, issues are addressed, and our operation fits in with the University's policies and goals.

Us: Are you involved hands-on with the review and publishing process?

EiC: The day-to-day activities are handled by Dr. Logan, the Managing Editor. He's the one who approves papers for publication, manages the review process, and collates reviewer feedback. I just review the outputs and give final approval for paper publication. Tom is very busy and unable to handle any further increase in workload. I would like to be more hands-on, but I'm also busy with strategic and administrative work myself. We're hoping your system will reduce Tom's workload so that he's not so stressed all the time.

Us: What are these outputs that you review and how do you review them?

EiC: Every paper is submitted to two peer reviews. Dr. Logan coordinates the feedback and necessary corrections and, once no more corrections are required, he emails me the paper, the reviewer's summary, and his recommendation. I review everything and I then approve or reject his recommendation, which is whether to publish the paper or not.

Us: Do you ever reject Dr Logan's recommendation?

EiC: It's extremely rare. I have confidence in my Managing Editor. Dr. Logan may be a bit eccentric, but he is very thorough in his work.

Us: How do you approve or reject a paper?

EiC: I just reply to the original email.

Us: Is your email digitally signed or encrypted?

EiC: Ermm…no, I suppose.

Us: So how would Dr. Logan know that the email is really from you? It's very easy to spoof emails.

EiC: Well, he assumes it is. Also, when I see him, we will usually mention it.

Us: I see. But Dr. Logan is currently away, so he won't be able to mention it in passing for the next 2 weeks at least.

EiC: Yes, I guess that's true.

Us: What would happen if we don't deliver the new system and you keep working the way you currently do?

EiC: Well for starters, I would have to hire another Managing Editor to ease Dr. Logan's workload. You don't know how hard it is to hire good MEs these days.

Us: Are you at all concerned with emailing potentially sensitive papers back and forth?

EiC: Indeed I am. We had an incident a few years back, where a reviewer emailed a paper with confidential data to the wrong person. Luckily, this was an honest person who notified us immediately and no damage was done. But this is a risk we are taking, if we continue working as we are.

Us: Thank you for your time, Professor Chakrabarti.

The IS Manager (ISM) interview

Us: Dr. Braddock, what is your role within this project?

ISM: As the University's IS manager, I am overseeing all IS system development and deployment. My main concerns are with security, compliance, and integration.

Us: Ok. Let's start with security. What are your security concerns?

ISM: Obviously, attaching sensitive files to email is inherently insecure. Also, I am concerned that some of these files, especially ones that support embedded macros, may be a carrier for viruses and other malicious code.

Us: Don't the editors and reviewers virus-scan the files?

ISM: They are supposed to, but you know how people are. They sometimes forget or are too busy to do so.

Us: OK. What about compliance?

ISM: The University prescribes a strict policy for auditing and reviewing the publication process. Currently, this policy is difficult to implement, as it means following a convoluted trail of emails and attachments. I would like the new system to make it easy to see what happened to a paper from its submission to its publication.

Us: Understood. And what are your integration concerns?

ISM: All university systems, like the one you will develop for Camford Press, need to be able to play well with **Camford University's Information System (CUIS)**. CUIS provides interfaces for user authentication, resource management, and other things besides.

Us: How do you envisage our system integrating with CUIS?

ISM: Well, if you're going to have user authentication, which I suspect you will have to, then it has to be through CUIS. We don't allow third-party identity services, such as Google or Twitter, to integrate with university systems.

Us: Thank you for your time, Dr. Braddock.

The Managing Editor (ME) email

We try to arrange a chat with Dr. Logan, the ME, but due to the time difference, this proves impossible. We then send him an email, asking him if he could tell us the following:

- What is his role in the review and publication process?

- Which part of this process would he like to see automated by our system?

- How does he hope our system will benefit him in his role?

- What would be the consequences for him as ME if our system was never delivered?

It is not until the following day that we receive a response from Dr. Logan:

> *Hello. Let me tell you, I can't wait for your system to be delivered. I have hardly time to eat or sleep nowadays. You can't imagine how hard it is to get two reviewers to review a paper within the same time period. I have to keep emailing people again and again. They are either too busy or just can't do the review within our deadlines. It's a nightmare I tell you. And don't get me started on checking each submitted paper just to make sure it adheres to our guidelines (I am attaching a copy of these, BTW). I have to do that every time an author submits a paper. It would be awesome if I didn't have to do that; it takes so much time.*

The rest of Dr. Logan's email turns out to be a long rant about traffic conditions where he is, so we can safely ignore that.

So, we have had input from all our client-side stakeholders and now it's time to try and make sense of what we learned.

Analyzing requirements

So far, we have captured requirements by having structured conversations with the EiC and the ISM. We also had an email communication from the ME. Let's now analyze these requirements in order to identify which requirement domain entities we are dealing with. We'll start by reviewing our interviews first. Structured conversations, like the ones we conducted, are the easiest way to identify requirement entities, as the structured conversation technique we have used is geared toward that purpose.

The EiC interview analysis

We first discovered the type of stakeholder we are dealing with. Professor Chakrabarti is a rare type of stakeholder, as she has business goals but is also an actor. When we asked her if she has hands-on involvement, she replied that she does the final review and gives approval. We also extracted her business goals by asking her what the risks are of continuing to use the current process, which are as follows:

- Preventing data and communication leaks. This damages the reputation of the business and can potentially cost money in lawsuits and so on. Preventing this is a very worthwhile goal.

- Avoiding having to hire new staff. Not only does hiring cost time and money, but in this case, hiring a new person may actually be very difficult. This is therefore a valid business goal.

There is also potentially a third goal, a domain goal, which is as follows:

- Simplify the EiC's final review and approval workflow.

As this would save the EiC's time, and therefore save the business money, this is a goal well-aligned with business needs.

We also gleaned some information about the ME's role and realized that the EiC's strategy for realizing her *Avoid hiring new staff* goal, is to make the ME's work easier and more productive.

After some thought, we come up with the capabilities needed to fulfill the EiC's goals. These are the ways in which the EiC's needs impact our system. The EiC needs to be able to do the following:

- Securely exchange messages and information. This will fulfill the *Preventing data and communications leaks* goal.

- Use a single point of access for final review and approval. This will stop the email back-and-forth and the downloading and opening of attachments. This will help fulfill the *Simplify the EiC's final review and approval workflow* goal.

There is also the goal of *Avoid hiring new staff*, but it seems we need to talk to Dr. Logan in order to derive the relevant capabilities, since this goal can be fulfilled by reducing his workload. So, for now, we create the discovered entities in our requirements model and move on to the next interview.

The ISM interview analysis

We quickly established that the ISM is a non-acting stakeholder as she won't be interacting in any way with our system. By asking about her potential concerns with our system, we quickly discerned her goals, which are as follows:

- Protect University systems from attack or corruption

- Ensure that systems can be comprehensively audited

- Ensure that applications are integrated with the University's IS systems

All of these are valid business goals, as they have obvious financial incentives. Let's see how our system could enable the ISM to achieve these goals. The capabilities we would need to provide would be the following:

- Automatically detect malicious or corrupt file submissions

- Provide an audit trail of every operation within our system

- Make our system users log in using the University's CUIS credentials.

We add these to our requirements model and move on to the next stakeholder we communicated with, Dr Logan, the ME. As we didn't have the chance to have a structured conversation with him, we'll have to do some extra work in order to identify his requirements.

The ME email analysis

First, let's reword the useful part of Dr. Logan's email in a more structured (and somewhat saner) manner:

- Two reviewers must review a paper within a limited time period.

- Reviewers are requested to perform reviews via email.

- Reviewers respond negatively or positively to a request for review.

- Authors submit papers (presumably by email).

- Dr. Logan checks submitted papers for adherence to guidelines.

- Dr. Logan wants to avoid checking submitted papers for adherence to guidelines.

- Dr. Logan wants to optimize the reviewer request and response process.

Now that we have a sanitized version of these requirements, we can apply the D3 technique in order to identify which requirement domain entities these requirements express.

Decomposing the ME's requirements

By applying the decomposition part of the D3 method, as detailed in *Chapter 5, Discovering and Analyzing Requirements*, in the *Techniques for analyzing requirements* section, we identify the requirement entities as explained in the subsequent sections.

Identifying actors

The people, or things, that interact with our system are as follows:

- Reviewer: A university academic in a specialized area who reviews papers in that area.

- Author: A graduate student or academic who wants to publish a written paper.

- Managing Editor (ME): The Camford Press staff responsible for daily editing activities.

Identifying capabilities

The impact the ME is having on our system consists of the following capabilities:

- Arranging reviews: The ME will be able to use our system to arrange reviews in a way that is quicker and more straightforward than it is at present.

- Detecting adherence to guidelines: The ME will be able to use our system to check for papers' adherence to guidelines in a more straightforward manner than at present.

Identifying features

The functionality required by the ME comprises the following features:

- Author submits paper
- Reviewer is asked to undertake a review
- Reviewer responds to a request for a review
- Reviewer reviews paper

Now that we have identified a number of requirement domain entities, let's take a look at how our requirements model looks right now:

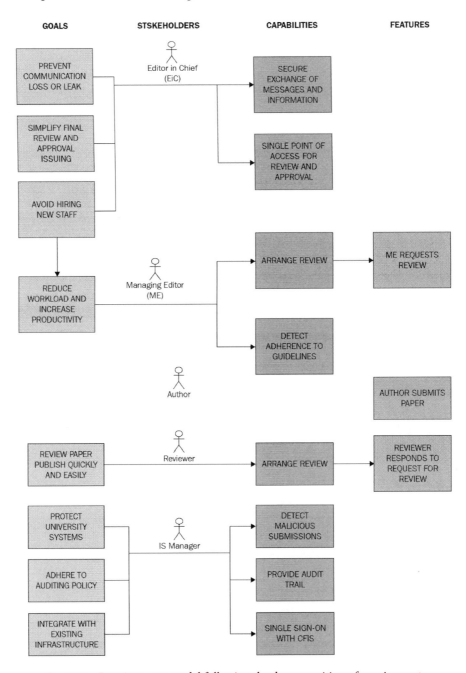

Fig. 10.1 – Requirements model following the decomposition of requirements

One thing to note is that we have duplicated the *Arrange Review* capability across both the scope of the reviewer and the ME. This is because this capability will enable both actors to do their job better. It is pretty obvious that in order to enable the ME to arrange reviews, we will need to implement the feature of requesting a review. It is similarly obvious that in order to enable the reviewer to arrange reviews, we will need to implement the feature of requesting a review.

Another thing of note is that we have identified a feature to allow the author to submit a paper. However, we still haven't fathomed out which capability this feature will help deliver. We write an action item to have a conversation with a number of authors. It is now time to refine our model by deriving some more requirements.

Deriving requirements

The purpose of this phase is to fill in any gaps in our requirements model. The only *orphaned* entity we currently have is the *Author submits paper* feature. We cannot really proceed with this until we understand what the author's expectations are. Luckily, Prof. Chakrabarti has kindly arranged a telephone chat with two authors who have previously published papers through Camford Press. Using the structured conversation techniques that we applied when chatting to the other stakeholders, we find that the author's main gripe with the current process is how long it takes to receive feedback and how unreliable it is, as sometimes emails don't get sent on time, or contain the wrong attachments and so on. When we ask them what they would like to achieve through the new system, they both reply that they want reliable notifications for their paper's progress status; that is, they want to know when it passes initial checking, when it has been reviewed by one or both reviewers, and when it has had final approval by the EiC.

Based on this, we add two goals for our authors: *Reduce paper review time* and *Receive timely status feedback*. We ascertain two capabilities needed to realize these goals: *Submit Paper* is the first one, as the author can't really reduce the review time unless they put their paper through our system. The other is *Receive progress notifications*, and this implies the proactive and timely push of paper status notifications to authors, as soon as they happen.

Now that we have a set of capabilities for all our stakeholders, let's identify some features that will help deliver these capabilities.

Discovering requirements

This is where we discover new requirement model entities, based on the entities we've already identified. Let's start with the ME. He needs to be able to arrange paper reviews from within our system and he would like the arranging of reviews to be easier and quicker than it currently is. The question is: what can the system offer in order to provide this capability in a way that helps achieve that goal? Lisa, our solutions architect, has an idea:

> *Instead of chasing the reviewers to see when they can do a review, why don't we have them register their availability with our system? Then, all that the ME has to do is select a time period and our system will tell him which reviewers are available at that time.*

We email this suggestion to Dr. Logan and, within hours, he responds by saying that this is an excellent idea and he would like this very much. We also approach a previous reviewer and we get the same positive response. We then create two new features to reflect this functionality: *Reviewer registers their availability* and *ME searches for available reviewers*.

Next, we turn our attention to the *Detect adherence to guidelines* Capability. After reading the guidelines document that Dr. Logan sent us, we realize that the main checkpoints are that the paper is written in English, that it has an abstract of up to 200 words, and that it contains a *conclusions and references* section. Tim, one of our developers, informs us that it is technologically feasible to scan a document's content, detect its language, check the presence and length of an abstract, and verify that certain sections exist. With that in mind, we create a new *Auto-scan paper* feature. Thinking a bit more about this feature, we come to a realization: this is a composite feature, that is, a feature composed of smaller, simpler sub-features, as described in *Chapter 4, Crafting Features Using Principles and Patterns*, in the *Discerning feature patterns* section. We replace this feature with four distinct, more narrowly-scoped features:

- Scan and parse paper content
- Check paper language
- Check paper abstract
- Check presence of mandatory sections

Finally, we apply some identifiers to our entities, as explained in *Chapter 6, Organizing Requirements*, in the *Assuring traceability with entity identifiers* section. Our requirements model now looks like this:

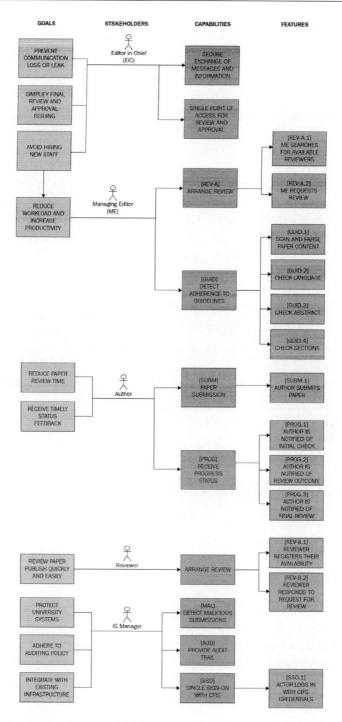

Fig. 10.2 – Requirements model following requirement derivation and discovery

> **Important tip**
>
> Many of the Non-Functional Requirements captured in our requirements model can be interpolated into other features. For instance, we could capture the behavior needed for the *Detect Malicious Submissions* capability by interpolating some steps to automatically scan the submitted files into our *Author submits paper* feature.

This is the same model we produced back in the *Decomposition* section, but it's now expanded and gaps between entities have been filled in. Our model is now much more comprehensive. We have a number of features that we can start fleshing out with scenarios. We also have a number of capabilities that don't have any features defined just yet. That's fine. Requirement analysis is an iterative and incremental process. Our model will keep changing quite frequently at first, but less frequently as our understanding increases. We are now ready for our second meeting with the stakeholders.

Planning the way forward

The second meeting with the stakeholders is arguably more important than the first. This is where, after having done our initial analysis, we present our requirements model and seek stakeholders' feedback and approval. This is also the meeting that kick-starts system development. We should now have enough features to have created a small, but perfectly-formed, system backlog (a list of all the features on our requirements model). Our objectives for the second meeting are as follows:

1. Explain the requirements model and get it approved by the stakeholders.

2. Present a first draft of our specification document, as detailed in *Chapter 6, Organizing Requirements*, in the *Creating a specification document* section.

3. Identify and discuss any areas of concern or ambiguity, if any.

4. Present and discuss potential risks, if any.

5. Identify a point of contact from our client-side stakeholders. We need one person to represent our client-side stakeholders so as to avoid ambiguity and noise.

6. Explain our analysis methodology and set up a schedule of regular review and discussion meetings. Ideally, we should be having bi-weekly meetings with the client-side stakeholders where we review the model, ascertain its relevance, and make any necessary modifications.

7. Explain our development life cycle, be that Scrum, Kanban, or something else, and ensure that stakeholders know when to expect software releases and when they need to review delivered features.

8. Review the backlog and prioritize features for development.

Regarding that last item, we ask Professor Chakrabarti which capabilities we should focus on first. She selects the following, as the most important and the least likely to change:

- Single sign-on
- Paper submission
- Guideline checks

We can now create our task board in preparation for development, and it looks like this:

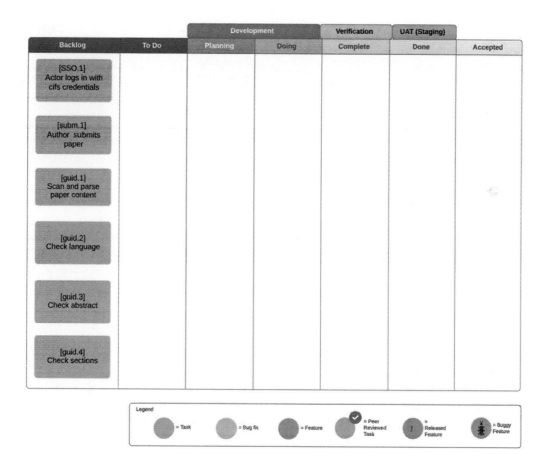

Fig 10.3 – Task board for the Camford Press system

Features related to the highest priority capabilities are near the top of our system backlog. Before starting development, our team will have a planning meeting where we will discuss which of these features to start working on first. We will define these features with detailed scenarios, as described in *Chapter 3, Writing Fantastic Features with Gherkin Language*, and then we will drag them to the *To Do* column, where these features will be constantly reviewed by our client-side point of contact in order to ensure that we capture the correct system behavior.

We can now begin our implementation, that is, software development. We may be using Scrum, Kanban (refer to *Chapter 7, Feature-First Development*), or some other agile framework or method to manage our implementation. Embarking on software development does not mean that our requirement management responsibilities are finished. We will be reviewing our requirements model on a regular basis with the stakeholders and we will be changing, creating, and removing domain entities as the project develops. We will also be constantly working with the stakeholders to select features from our backlog, describe them so that they are fully-formed, and move them to our To-Do list when we are ready to start implementing them. Luckily, the previous chapters in this book detail exactly how to do all the above, so we are well equipped to handle our project as it iteratively and incrementally evolves from some vague needs and wishes to a fully functioning system that works as intended. We are well on our way to making our stakeholders' requirements a reality!

Summary

In this chapter, we put our previous learning into the context of starting a *real* project. Knowing all the techniques, methods, and processes needed to manage requirements and create specifications is very important, but there are other, less tangible aspects of working on a software project that can make a difference. The first two meetings with our client's stakeholders are critical. The first meeting (I call it **first contact**) is where we establish communication channels and start managing expectations. This is where we start getting a real feel for what our clients expect and desire from our system. After our first meeting, we should be working to produce the outline of a requirements model, which we will open up for feedback to all our stakeholders.

Having our requirements model and specification scrutinized regularly builds trust and confidence between us and the stakeholders. This is why that second client meeting is so important, because it establishes all these steps that foster transparency and communication early enough in the project.

The other thing that this chapter aims to emphasize is the importance of avoiding the *waterfall* trap. Just like agile software development, agile requirement elicitation, analysis, and modelling is something that happens iteratively and incrementally. Trying to extract every single detail and get a complete picture at the beginning of a project is futile. Many of these fine details can only be derived when both we and our client have a better understanding of what our system will do and how it will do it. Things will be changing often, but being agile means being able to manage change. This is why, in our first project meeting, we don't even try to nail down every detail, just get a high-level overview. We can then analyze requirements in our own time and attend our second meeting with a requirements model that will serve as the starting point of a continuous conversation between us and the stakeholders. Our understanding of the requirements and the requirements model evolve in parallel, one leading the other.

So, we have reached the end of the chapter and of this book. I hope you enjoyed reading it and that the information contained herein will help you deliver successful software systems, with minimum risk and maximum efficiency, just as it has helped me do over the years. Cheers to successful systems and happy clients!

Other Books You May Enjoy

If you enjoyed this book, you may be interested in these other books by Packt:

Modern Computer Architecture and Organization

Jim Ledin

ISBN: 978-1-83898-439-7

- Get to grips with transistor technology and digital circuit principles
- Discover the functional elements of computer processors
- Understand pipelining and superscalar execution
- Work with floating-point data formats
- Understand the purpose and operation of the supervisor mode
- Implement a complete RISC-V processor in a low-cost FPGA
- Explore the techniques used in virtual machine implementation
- Write a quantum computing program and run it on a quantum computer

Solutions Architect's Handbook

Saurabh Shrivastava and Neelanjali Srivastav

ISBN: 978-1-83864-564-9

- Explore the various roles of a solutions architect and their involvement in the enterprise landscape

- Approach big data processing, machine learning, and IoT from an architect's perspective and understand how they fit into modern architecture

- Discover different solution architecture patterns such as event-driven and microservice patterns

- Find ways to keep yourself updated with new technologies and enhance your skills

- Modernize legacy applications with the help of cloud integration

- Get to grips with choosing an appropriate strategy to reduce cost

Leave a review - let other readers know what you think

Please share your thoughts on this book with others by leaving a review on the site that you bought it from. If you purchased the book from Amazon, please leave us an honest review on this book's Amazon page. This is vital so that other potential readers can see and use your unbiased opinion to make purchasing decisions, we can understand what our customers think about our products, and our authors can see your feedback on the title that they have worked with Packt to create. It will only take a few minutes of your time, but is valuable to other potential customers, our authors, and Packt. Thank you!

Index

Symbols

80-20 rule 62, 63

A

active verb 90
actors
  about 5
  detecting 90
Agile requirements management workflow
  applying 163
  Development, Validation,
    & Verification 167
  Elicitation and Analysis phase 163, 164
  executable specification 166
  Modeling and Discovery phase 165
Agile SDLC 107, 108
anti-patterns
  about 71
  compound steps 76
  incidental details 73
  scenario flooding 74
  thinking like developers 72
  vague outcomes 74, 75
automated verification
  need for 138

automated verification code patterns
  leveraging 142
automation code
  layering, to avoid brittleness 138

B

background
  about 38
  used, for avoiding step repetition 49
BDD life cycle
  stages 31
BDD principles
  applying 62
behavior-driven development (BDD)
  about 14, 30, 62
  with impact mapping 32
brittle step definition problem 139, 140
browser details
  hiding, with Page Object
    pattern 143-145
bugs 110
Business Analysis Body of
    Knowledge (BABOK)
  reference link 156
business goals 8, 9

business process
  about 96
  for order approvals 97
business process mapping
  guidelines 98
business requirements 156

C

Camford conundrum 170
Camford University's Information
    System (CUIS) 173
capability
  about 22, 24
  detecting 91
  examples 24
  identifying 23
capability, versus feature
  about 25
  association 26
  atomicity 26
  directly actionable 26
  granularity 26
  key action 26
  key question 26
  point of view 26
cards 111
Change Requests (CRs) 128
completed Sprint 126
complex operations
  wrapping up, with Façade
      Pattern 146, 147
composite features pattern 66-68
constraints 33
content rating requisites
  for knowledge-sharing platform 27, 28
Continuous Integration and Continuous
    Delivery (CI/CD) 120

CRUD Features pattern 65, 66

D

Data Tables
  used, for avoiding repetition 44
  versus Scenario Outlines 48
Decompose, Derive, Discover (D3) 89
decomposition
  about 90
  outcome 93
derivation
  about 94
  outcome 94
discovery
  about 95
  outcome 95, 96
domain entities 3
domain goals
  about 7
  examples 7
Domain Layer 141
Draw.io
  URL 102

E

Editor-in-Chief (EiC) interview 171-173
EiC interview analysis 175
emergent bug 129, 130
employees
  onboarding 28, 29
entity identifiers
  used, for ensuring traceability 103, 104
Equifax 6
executable specifications 31
Experian 6

F

Façade Pattern
  complex operations, wrapping
    up 146, 147
feature
  about 22, 24, 30, 38
  detecting 91
  examples 24, 25
  executable specifications 55-58
  identifying 23
  purposes 39
  tags, using for 54, 55
  writing, tips 52
  writing, with Gherkin 39-41
feature creep 132
Feature-First approach 167
feature interpolation pattern 68-71
Feature Title 38
five whys technique 8
fully formed Feature
  writing 50-52
functional requirements
  versus non-functional requirements 32

G

Gherkin
  features, writing 39-41
  reference link 39
GitMind
  URL 102
glossary 85-87
Goal-Capability-Feature Impact
  Map model 68
goals
  about 13, 20
  case study, on lack of strategy 10

case study, on specifying tactics 11
detecting 91
identifying 7

H

high-level features 23
high-performance capability 33

I

impact 38
impact mapping
  about 20
  benefits 21
impact maps
  about 20, 21
  modeling requisites 20
incomplete Sprint 127, 128
IS Manager (ISM) interview 173
ISM interview analysis 176

J

just-in-time development
  actualizing 119, 120

K

Kanban
  dealing, with changes 135
  working with 132, 133
Kanban boards 116
Kanban development cycle 134, 135
Kanban planning 133
knowledge-sharing platform
  content rating requisites 27, 28

L

low-level features 23
Lucidchart
  URL 102

M

Managing Editor (ME) email 174
ME email analysis 176
ME's requirements, decomposing
  about 177
  actors, identifying 177
  capabilities, identifying 177
  features, identifying 177, 179
MindMup
  URL 102
modeling requisites
  with impact maps 20

N

non-acting stakeholders 6
non-functional requirements
  about 33
  areas 33
  impact map 34
  versus functional requirements 32
notes 38

O

Operational Layer 141

P

Page Object pattern
  browser details, hiding 143-145

Pareto principle 62
passive verb 90
patterns
  discerning, in features 64
  implementation details, separating
    from operational details 148, 149
  selecting 147, 148
polysemy 85
primary actors 6
processing 85
product backlog
  about 108
  creating 107
  on task board 112
publishing 85

Q

quality attributes 33

R

requirements
  about 2, 3, 13
  analyzing 87, 174
  business requirements 156
  classifying 156
  dealing, with changes to
    requirements 159-162
  deriving 179
  discovering 180, 182
  documenting 157
  examples 91, 92
  life cycle 4, 5
  modeling 153, 155
  prioritizing 157, 158
  prioritizing, by cost 158
  prioritizing, by risk 158

prioritizing, by urgency 158
prioritizing, by value 157
solution requirements 156
stakeholders requirements 156
transition requirements 156
turning, into specifications 14
validating 153
verifying 159
requirements analysis
preparing for 82
requirements domain model 2
requirements elicitation
about 80-82, 171
initial discussions, leading 171
requirements funnel 14, 15
requirements funneling 14
requirements management
life cycle 152
requirements model
easy access, providing to 102
return on investment (ROI) 158
reviewer 90

S

Scenario Outlines
used, for avoiding repetition 46-48
versus Data Tables 48
Scenarios
about 38, 39
adding 45, 46
discovering 42-44
observations 53
scripting 41
scope creep 132
Scrum
working with 120
Scrum artifacts 121

Scrum boards 116
Scrum events 121
Scrum Guide
reference link 118
Scrum team 120
secondary actors 6
Service Level Agreements (SLAs) 33
Service Request Manager (SRM) 132
SMART goals
about 11
case study, on less time on
support calls 12
case study, on reducing cost 12
Software Development Life
Cycle (SDLC) 107
solution requirements 156
specification
about 3, 13
creating 155, 156
scoping 106
stakeholder agreement,
obtaining on 106
specification document
creating 104, 105
Sprint
about 120
changes, to existing behavior 131
completed Sprint 126
dealing, with change 128, 129
development cycle 122-125
emergent bugs 129, 130
end of Sprint 125
incomplete Sprint 127, 128
Sprint backlog 122
Sprint planning 121
staging environment
creating 116

stakeholder agreement
  obtaining, on specification 106
stakeholder model 82-84
stakeholders
  about 20
  discovering 84
  identifying 5, 6
stakeholders requirements 156
strategic goals 9, 10
structured conversation 88, 89
successful delivery
  setting up, for system capabilities 116
synonymizing 85
system behavior 63, 64
system builders 2

T

tags
  using, for features 54
task board
  creating 116-118
tasks 109
Technical Layer 142
traceability
  ensuring, with entity identifiers 103, 104
transition requirements 156

U

user story 16, 38
user-story hell 80

V

verification code
  layers of abstraction, adding 140-142

X

XMind
  URL 102

Printed in Great Britain
by Amazon